The GIFT BASKET DESIGN BOOK

Everything You Need to Know to Create Beautiful, Professional-Looking Gift Baskets for All Occasions

SHIRLEY GEORGE FRAZIER

The Globe Pequot Press

GUILFORD, CONNECTICUT

Text design: M. A. Dubé
Photo credits: All photos are courtesy of the author.

ISSN 1548-1557
ISBN 0-7627-2795-0

Manufactured in the United States of America

First Edition/Second Printing

*To John, Genesis, Mom, Cassandra,
and Aunt Shirley, the loves of my life.*

*To all of the designers, store owners, and product
manufacturers who have helped to make gift baskets
a worldwide phenomenon.*

CONTENTS

INTRODUCTION

Why I Began Making Gift Baskets

Mix a cup of entrepreneurial ancestors with one clever spouse, and what do you get? Ideas that spawn enough creativity to last a lifetime. When I began searching for a career that provided satisfaction, gift baskets never entered the picture. I trained to be a secretary, but I soon found working for someone else to be boring. In ten years I worked for ten different companies. So I began searching for a profession that would challenge my creativity.

My great-grandmother Mary Smith grew her own strawberries in Virginia and shipped them to Manhattan during the early 1900s. In the 1940s a great-aunt made fudge, and my mother was her delivery person. My father was co-owner of a chemical company in the 1970s. Their pursuits sealed my fate as an entrepreneur, but you don't have to find creativity in your family to be bitten by the gift basket bug. What most designers share is a love of making something beautiful with their hands. If you possess this trait, you'll love gift baskets.

My mother enrolled me in sewing classes when I was ten. I knitted and crocheted in my teen years, and I've always loved arts and crafts. You couldn't pry me away from making jack o'lanterns at camp. Were you the same way? That's part of what gift basket designers have in common.

In the 1980s computers were becoming a hot commodity. I wanted to start a word processing service, but I quickly gave up that idea and replaced it with one to open an intimate apparel boutique. I'm fascinated by retailing and have worked in small and large stores. Since ladies love lingerie, it seemed to be a good match. Then my husband, John, made a gift for a coworker. He took a small bottle of liqueur and paired it with a shot glass, gluing rocks to the bottom. He covered it in plastic wrap and added a small bow on top. The recipient loved it. John's thoughtfulness is what led me to a career making gift baskets.

If you're interested in making one single gift basket, that's fine. But if you want to keep your hands constantly submerged in the shred and cellophane, you can do that, too. There's always a birthday or celebration where a gift basket is welcomed. We also make baskets to apologize for an error, help folks get back on their feet, and bring comfort in times of grief.

My design ideas were somewhat strange at the beginning. For instance, I thought a gift for people who were afraid of dental work would be popular. Instead of using a basket, I'd use a giant, hollow enamel tooth cut in half with a hinge in the back to hold it together so that gift items could be placed between the two parts. Another idea was to calm individuals afraid of airplane travel. A miniature suitcase would hold items (cards, dice, puzzle books, and so on) that kept people busy en route.

Choosing containers rather than baskets is part of the creativity. I've always been captivated by unique containers, because it sets the gift apart from traditional baskets. That's what drew people to my designs. A dish drainer housed the new-home gift, a child's wagon welcomed the new baby, and a miniature rocking chair symbolized retirement, all holding gifts and snacks for the receiver.

Baskets are more beautiful today than when I started designing. Some are made with wire, and others contain sophisticated trim or hardware. It can be difficult to choose a vessel because each one is more gorgeous than the next.

Gift baskets are a joy to make, and anything goes, as long as you can piece it together. Being creative is fun, but sometimes a design is so large and challenging that it takes hours to make. Some of us will sit back and marvel over it when completed. Others will critique it to death, fixing this and that to the point that we take the whole thing apart and start all over again. That's how passionately designers feel about gift baskets, and I'm excited to share the passion with you.

Before we get started, let me introduce you to some words you'll find throughout this book. Many are used interchangeably, and I want to ensure that you understand each meaning.

- *Baskets, containers,* and *vessels* represent the same thing. All three words refer to the products that hold the contents you've chosen for your designs.
- *Cavity* refers to the inside opening of a basket or container. It's the area filled with packing paper or tissue-covered floral foam.
- *Cellophane, cello, plastic film,* and *closure material* describe the product that encloses the basket, protecting the contents until the recipient removes it to enjoy the contents.
- *Contents, product,* and *item* refer to anything that is placed within a

basket, container, or vessel. This includes, but is not limited to, snacks, gifts, shred, and enhancements.

- *Enhancements* and *embellishments* have similar meanings and describe the flora and fauna added to your baskets.
- *Floral foam, Sahara,* and *brick* share the same meaning.
- A *gift basket designer* is also known as a *pro* or *professional.*
- *Gifts* are items that are inedible. Examples include stationery, coasters, and cookbooks.

- The *receiver* or *recipient* is the person for whom the gift is being made.
- *Snacks* refers to anything that can be eaten or swallowed. Popcorn, chocolates, and coffee are part of this category.

Whether you make gift baskets for fun or want to take your skill further and start a business, this book will provide you with many ideas to create beautiful gift baskets for everyone in your life.

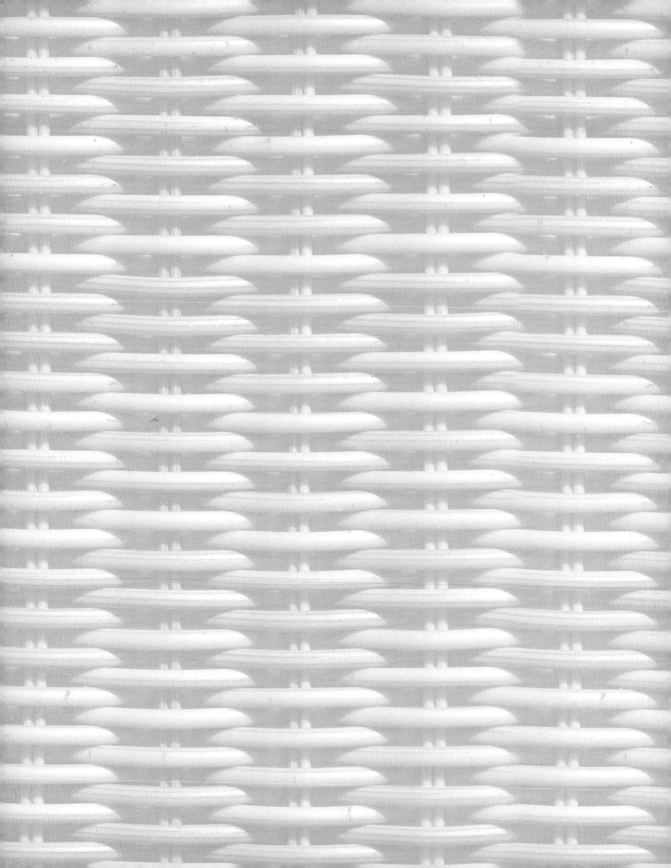

PART ONE
Design Basics

More than just a present, a gift basket is a mood-altering experience.

Chapter 1

HUMBLE BEGINNINGS, FABULOUS FUTURE

Creating a Work of Art for Every Occasion

It happens every time I teach a gift basket design class. The group of aspiring beginners stares at the disorder in front of them, wondering how this seemingly broken puzzle will be pieced together. Silence reigns as the students concentrate on filling their baskets with chocolates, chips, bottled water, and other goods. The peace is shattered by the crunch of paper among twenty pairs of hands, all filling their baskets simultaneously. Someone snaps a skewer into three pieces. Fingers tuck shred neatly between products that stand tall like soldiers. Clear cellophane bags rattle as they're shimmied around and above each new creation, soon to be closed and topped with a dazzling, handmade bow.

Then, one by one, the new designers gasp and admire the masterpieces before them. What emerges from controlled chaos is a group of individuals who've completed their first lesson in professional gift basket design. They smile broadly and

are eager to learn more. But first, they notice something unexpected. Each person was given the same products, yet every basket looks different. How could something that started out the same end up looking so dissimilar? The answer lies in two words: *individual creativity.*

Every designer, whether beginner or expert, has a vision of how to make a gift basket. The construction always changes, even when making multiples of the same design. That's what makes this bundle so fascinating and such a joy to make or receive. And there's always something new and exciting to unleash your creative genius.

A QUICK HISTORY LESSON

I thought gift baskets were a fairly new phenomenon when I started making them in 1989. Magazines on the topic had yet

3

to be published, and videos were non-existent. All those who were making baskets kept their design skills a closely guarded secret.

Little did I know that the gift basket dates back to at least 1913, when it was first mentioned in *Woman's Home Companion,* a magazine that's reminiscent of today's supermarket journals. The article "Baskets for the New Baby" included photographs of baskets and suggested baby gift items—bibs, brushes, combs, soaps, and powders. There was no mention of wrapping everything in cellophane, but the idea was there, and uncovering it was monumental for me.

House of Wembdon, a New York–based toiletries manufacturer, advertised its gift basket sets in *The New Yorker* in 1937. Its baskets ranged in price from $1.50 to $5.00, and the price of a jumbo-sized $15.00 basket must have seemed like a king's ransom during the Depression.

A 1943 article in the magazine *House Beautiful* proclaimed gift baskets as "something to give the rich." The Christmas baskets were themed for cocktail parties, potluck dinners, and Asian cuisine and ranged in price from $7.00 to $11.50. Some of the contents, mixed nuts and popcorn, are still popular today, while anchovy fillets and turkey a la king have fallen out of favor.

Gift baskets were a favorite of *Sunset,* a California lifestyles magazine, which frequently showed designs on its pages. One 1956 article titled "How to Pack a Gift Basket" featured a step-by-step guide on combining fresh fruits with canned and jarred foods. It also showed how to add cellophane and a bow.

I gathered this history in the summer of 2000 while searching through the New York Public Library archives. Photos, advertisements, and articles appeared in magazines that were so old they nearly disintegrated when I touched them. Gift baskets have stood the test of time, through high and low economies. And the myth about gift baskets being a new industry faded almost as fast as it began.

WHY GIFT BASKETS ARE POPULAR

If you give someone a picture frame, it's a gift. But when you present the same person with a gift basket consisting of the frame surrounded by candles, bath salts, a music CD, body powder, and lotion, you give a mood-altering experience. You wait to see the expression on the recipient's face—the pleasure and excitement all at once. That's what separates presenting a gift basket from the mere act of giving a gift.

Don't be surprised if the receiver doesn't open your gift basket—ever. For some, the creation is too exquisite to disturb. This has happened to me numerous times. I'll fill an order and deliver it if it's not too far from my workshop. The recipients are overjoyed and ask me to come in and sit for a while. I wonder if I have a

Many basket recipients don't open their gifts—ever.

telling them what's inside and noting if the food products aren't eaten within a specified period, they'll no longer be edible. Other times you might consider placing a label on the bottom stating this fact as a reminder.

I love it when a person enjoys the basket's contents, and I also consider it an honor to make a design that becomes a collector's item. Some designers don't feel the same way. They want the person to open and eat or use the contents. But should you make the recipient part with such beauty? After you've designed and delivered the basket, it's okay to let go of your "baby" and move on to other designs.

People never tire of receiving gift baskets. The vessel is different, the contents change, the embellishments depict the occasion or season, and there's always a surprise inside. No other gift promises such delight. That's why you're ready to make your own, and I'll show you how.

You'll find making gift baskets to be fun and rewarding. Perhaps you are looking for general knowledge about this skill, or maybe you know how to make baskets but want to elevate your expertise. This book will help you do both. First you'll learn about the supplies and tools needed in your workspace. Then we'll get into design techniques that the pros have mastered. I can't wait to start.

trustworthy face, or is it that I've presented them with a treasure and they want to share this joyful moment? Sometimes I can stay a while, and other times I must rush off to another delivery.

If I stay, it's not uncommon for the recipients to place the gift on a table with other decorative items and state that it will sit there forever. For some, the memory of receiving the basket is more significant than the contents. What's really important is that the receivers love what you've created. You may find yourself

Start with a sturdy wooden basket of any color or size.

Chapter 2

BASIC SUPPLIES

Everything You Need to Design Beautiful Baskets

Most of us are mesmerized when we see gift baskets in boutiques, specialty shops, and department stores. Their composition reveals a well-thought-out selection of foods and gifts surrounded by clear or colorful packaging. What we don't see is the construction hidden underneath.

Gift-basket-building techniques aren't always simple, but designers use the same products in creative ways to support each piece. Gift baskets are created with a collection of items, some of which you're familiar with and others that you've probably seen in a craft store but never knew how to use. After combining everything together to form a gift basket, you'll step back and wonder why you waited so long to create your first masterpiece.

THE ESSENTIALS

Here's a look at the items you'll consider buying to make your first basket. You'll find sources for all the items mentioned here listed in the Resource section at the end of this book.

An Attractive Basket

Select a basket of any color and size that's made with a sturdy wood frame. Make sure that the basket's weave is smooth and unbroken on all sides as well as on the bottom and handle. When placed on the floor, a well-made basket sits flat and doesn't wobble. Your first basket, whether square, round, oval or rectangular, should include a handle.

A basket with a depth of 4 to 5 inches is a good size for practice. It will give you enough space to create a design that includes five to six items. Also, it's best not to select a plastic basket such as the type used by a child for Easter egg hunting. A tightly-woven basket made from wood is the vessel of choice to create a design that looks like it was made by a professional.

Tip: Add color to an unpainted wooden basket by spraying it with non-toxic paint in an aerosol can. Apply the paint outside your home, if possible, or in a well-ventilated space. Use gloves and a pair of goggles to reduce hazards and cleanup.

Crumpled paper is used to fill a basket's interior.

Shred provides a colorful cushion between the basket and its contents.

Open-and-eat snacks are favorite gift basket items.

Newspaper or Packing Paper

Single sheets of crumpled paper are used to fill the basket's inside opening. Newspaper is a popular item that many designers choose, but some are against it because the ink can transfer from paper to hands. An alternative is to use packing paper. This plain paper, usually packaged in boxes to protect mail-order items, is tan, beige, or brown in color. It is rigid and more voluminous than newspaper, so less is needed to fill the inside basket.

Commercial packaging stores and wholesale gift basket suppliers (listed in the Resource section) sell packing paper on a roll, but to save money you can start saving the packing paper that comes in packages you receive from mail-order companies. Old wrapping paper is another alternative. Styrofoam peanuts can also be used, but they are less desirable because they can move inside the basket, making the foods and gifts shift unexpectedly.

Shred

Every basket contains shred. It's a material most often made from wood or paper and molded into various forms. That's why shred has many names—parchment, excelsior, Mylar, tissue, and sizzle (also known as crinkle).

Some shreds are coarse and stiff, while others are soft and spongy. All of them provide a colorful cushion on top of the

newspaper or packing paper, in between the basket and snacks. Your choice of shred depends on what you like and what looks best in the design.

Snacks and Foods

The basket's contents are the main attraction—that's what makes people melt with delight. The most popular snack items are:

- Chocolates
- Cookies
- Popcorn
- Potato chips
- Pretzels
- Nuts
- Crackers
- Cheese
- Beef sausage
- Jams and jellies
- Coffee, cocoa, and tea

There are many other products to select, but these items are chosen most often because each can be opened and eaten immediately, giving the recipient instant gratification. Another reason for this group's popularity is that you can design many themes with these same products. All of them are great for birthdays, thank-you gifts, housewarmings, and other everyday events. Each product is prepackaged and ready for purchasing at local stores, which is why open-and-eat snacks are the best items to fill your baskets.

Fact: Some cheeses need refrigeration, but others can be stored in a cabinet or

Use flowers and picks to add interest.

Enclose your baskets in plain or printed cellophane or bags.

Add bows for a gorgeous enhancement.

container. Cheeses made with preservatives that allow them to be kept at room temperature are just as delicious as the refrigerated kind.

Silk Flowers and Picks

You don't have to be a botanist to select flowers that create a soft and pretty appearance inside the basket. Flowers are the long-stemmed beauties that are added to the back and sides of the basket, while picks are short (with approximately 2-inch stems) and placed in the front.

Daisies, gyp (gypsophila), pansies, and violets are four great choices, but that's not all. Look at the different varieties at your local craft store. Determine which flowers and picks will enhance your designs without overwhelming the foods and gifts.

Cellophane or Basket Bag

A basket and its contents are enclosed in a thin plastic film that keeps the design in place until it's opened. Cellophane is available on a wide roll, usually 20, 30, or 40 inches in width and 25, 50, or 100 feet long. Basket bags are precut to fit many basket sizes and shapes. Cellophane and bags are made in a clear film or decorated with flowers, fruit, hearts, dots, phrases, and other prints.

Another way to close your gift baskets is to use shrink wrap, which is described later in this chapter.

Premade and Handmade Bows

A pretty bow tied around the closing at the top (also known as the neck) of a basket complements the attractive design. Premade bows are easy to use and available in many sizes, colors, and styles. They are purchased flat, but when the two slim ribbons wound into the bow are pulled, a gorgeous enhancement takes shape.

Handmade bows are fashioned from spooled ribbon. There are videos and tabletop machines available at retail stores and on the Internet (sources are listed in the Resource section) to teach you how to make your own bows.

Look at all the available ribbon and bow styles at craft stores before making your choice. One basket may look best with a solid-colored bow tie, while another will sparkle when topped with a large multicolored puff bow.

Scissors and Other Supplies

You will be cutting many items such as cellophane and tissue paper, so a good pair of shears is essential to creating great designs.

Your scissors must be sharp, and that means investing in a sharpening tool or outside sharpener (craft or knife store retailer). This will ensure quick cutting the first time, as well as preventing any injuries that may result in medical attention. Some designers also use small, all-purpose cutters or electric scissors when

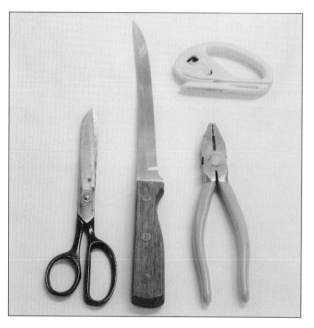

Sharp cutting tools are critical to the basket maker.

Transparent tape secures cellophane around the basket.

Basket keepsakes will be appreciated long after the basket is gone.

cutting cellophane for orders in excess of a hundred baskets.

A sharp knife is handy if you plan to cut floral foam to place inside of your baskets, as you'll learn in chapter 3. As with scissors, one clean cut into the foam will keep your design time to a minimum.

Wire cutters are perfect for flowers, picks and other enhancements with overly long stems. Such stems should be cut before they're included in a basket. Scissors are ruined by running them over the thick wire, so wire cutters are the best solution. Craft and gift basket suppliers sell these tools. Read the packaging to determine which wire cutters to buy before making your choice.

Keep a roll of transparent tape handy. It's needed to secure cellophane around the basket, and you'll use it for other tasks as well.

MORE HELPFUL PRODUCTS

The items from the previous groups form the basis for designing your gorgeous gift baskets. But there's more to review before you start. If you want to include heavy bottles such as cider and syrups in your baskets, there are special supplies to consider buying for extra support. They will help you anchor, secure, and add interest to your designs. Here are some additions to the basic supplies.

Gifts

Not all baskets are made solely with snacks. There are many fun and thoughtful keepsake items that are perfect for baskets. These include:

- Gift books
- Bath and body products
- Mugs
- Stationery and writing instruments
- Key chains
- Cookbooks
- Candles
- Utensils
- Picture frames
- Napkins
- Plush toys
- Plant seeds
- Gardening tools
- Baby items
- Drinking glasses
- Antistress toys

Gifts are very popular, so consider adding these items in your gift baskets as a memento that will be around when the snacks are gone.

Floral Foam

Floral foam is another way to help stabilize snacks and gifts inside the basket. It is gray and shaped like a brick but is very lightweight. Also known as Sahara, it's a dry material that's gritty to the touch. It is used most often by florists to support silk flower arrangements.

Another way to stabilize your gifts is with floral foam.

Use tissue paper to cover floral foam.

Any number of embellishments can add sparkle to your creations.

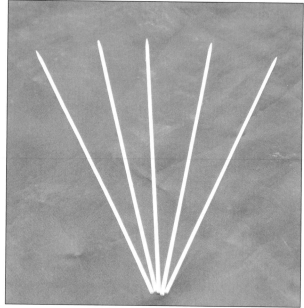

Skewers allow your gift items to stand upright.

Do not confuse floral foam with Oasis, which is usually green in color. Although both products are rectangular in shape, Oasis acts as a sponge to hold water when soaked and is used to preserve fresh flowers and plants.

Tip: Use a long knife to carve the floral foam so that it fits snugly just below the basket's rim. Trim the foam sparingly so as not to cut too much at one time. You'll see this technique in chapter 3.

Tissue Paper

If you use floral foam, it must be covered with tissue paper before placing it inside the basket. The tissue keeps the foam from transferring onto the receiver's hands or clothes. Tissue also acts as a shield between the foam and the snacks and gifts placed on top of it. Any tissue paper color is acceptable because it will be hidden from view once the basket is completed.

Another use for tissue paper is as a barrier between the packing paper and basket. This is needed when a basket contains an open weave, allowing the packing paper to be exposed. An example is shown in chapter 3.

Embellishments

Why add only flowers to baskets when there are so many decorative items to choose from? Stroll through the aisles of a local craft store, and you'll see more alternatives that will add a creative touch.

What all embellishments have in common is that each is supported by a long, slim stem. Among the decorative touches to look for are butterflies, frosted balloons, onion grass, and picks (mentioned earlier under "Silk Flowers and Picks"). You'll see how to add embellishments in chapter 5.

Bamboo Skewers

These long, thin polished pieces of wood aren't just for the barbecue. Skewers are paired with floral foam to make snacks and gifts magically stand straight. The top third of a skewer is attached with transparent tape to the front, back, or side of a snack or gift item. The bottom of the skewer is inserted into the foam. The snack or gift will stand upright inside the basket with help from the skewer. You'll see this simple technique in chapter 4.

Double-Coated Tape

Why would anyone need tape that's sticky on both sides? This is what designers use to hide skewers from sight. When a skewer is secured with transparent tape onto a snack or gift, it must be masked so that no one sees the anchoring technique.

Place double-coated tape on top of the transparent tape. Then press a pinch of shred atop the double-coated tape, and

Double-sided tape is another designers' secret.

A heat gun and shrink wrap will give you a tighter package.

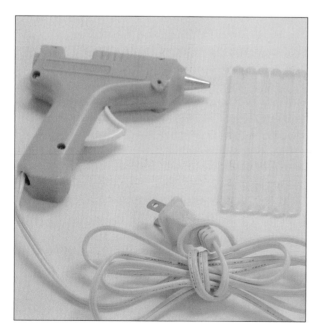

A hot glue gun and glue sticks bond enhancements to the outer wrap.

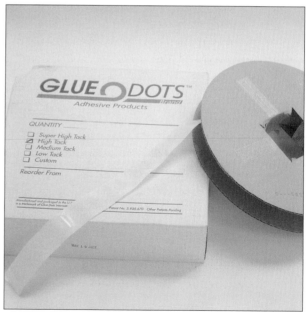

Glue dots bond items together within the basket.

the skewer vanishes, leaving everyone to wonder "How do you do that?" This will also be shown in chapter 4.

Shrink Wrap

Cellophane and basket bags provide what's called a soft wrap around a gift basket. But if you prefer a tight, crystal-clear appearance, shrink wrap will provide it. Shrink wrap is the closing material that most retail stores select. A machine dispenses the wrap, and a heat gun shrinks and seals the wrap around the design.

Craft stores also sell shrink wrap on rolls and in shell formats (shrink wrap bags with rounded top edges), eliminating the need for the shrink wrap machine. Both are priced for the budget-conscious designer. With each product, you'll need to use a heat gun to shrink the film around the basket.

In lieu of a professional heat gun, some new designers shrink the wrap with a hair dryer. You may find that your home dryer's settings are better for hair than for shrink wrap, but this is the time to experiment. If the hair dryer doesn't work to your specifications, a low-cost heat gun is a worthwhile investment. Chapter 6 will show you shrink-wrapping techniques.

Hot Glue Gun

Enhancements such as flowers, ribbons, and bows sometimes need extra support to stay in place. Glue sticks are inserted into a hot glue gun, which turns the hard glue into a liquid. The softened glue that is pressed from the gun creates a bond between the embellishment and the chosen surface.

Hot glue is used between cellophane and ribbon to create a rippled effect on the outside of the basket, or it can keep flowers securely in place on the cellophane. Use hot glue safely and responsibly. Once applied, it is difficult to remove.

Glue Dots

Here's a product you can use instead of or in addition to a hot glue gun. Glue dots are preformed sticky circles that bond two or more things together. These puffy, neutral-colored dots are available in varied forms of stickiness (tacky, very tacky, and highly tacky). They're dispensed on a roll and ready to join anything within the basket. Unlike hot glue, these dots are easily removed from any surface.

Curling Ribbon

This thin, wavy ribbon wrapped on 5-inch spools is most often added around the neck of a basket where the main bow holds the outside wrapping (cellophane, basket bag, or what have you) in place.

Once the curling ribbon is tied and knotted, the ends hang downward. These ends can be curled with scissors or a

Curling ribbon closes and embellishes the outer wrap.

ribbon cutter to create a curly-haired effect around the basket.

Tip: Tie several curling ribbon colors around the basket's neck to add extra pizzazz to the design.

These additional items will become as important to you as the basic gift-basket-making products. One of the best things about making gift baskets is that very little is thrown away. For example, old cellophane can be used to fill an empty basket opening instead of or in addition to newspaper or packing paper. Embellishments that tear or break apart are easily added in a different area of the basket (shown in chapter 11). There are other ways to recycle old and worn-out supplies that I'll share with you throughout this book. First, however, you need to learn where to find gift basket supplies.

WHERE TO FIND SUPPLIES

Gift basket snacks, gifts, and enhancements line the aisles of many stores that you currently visit.

Craft stores such as Michaels, Ben Franklin, A. C. Moore, and Treasure Island sell many of the supplies that complete your gift basket designs, including vast selections of baskets, shred, flowers, bows, curling ribbon, tissue paper, and other tools. Search each aisle thoroughly to view all your options. Inspect the baskets stacked on tiered shelves and in bins. Familiarize yourself with the flowers, pore over the ribbon selections, and see all the available shreds. If you've never combed through a craft store, you'll find this first outing to be a fun and enlightening experience.

Before buying new baskets, look around your own home for vessels that you've collected in years past. Some attics and basements harbor elegant woven creations that will now be put to good use. Your search may also reveal other stored items that will enhance your designs.

Tip: Live in a rural area? Use pinecones found in your backyard instead of buying them from a craft store. Once the basket is filled, pinecones are used as an enhancement along the basket's inside rim. Microwave the cones individually for one to two minutes to rid them of microscopic organisms, or heat them in an oven at 400 degrees for five to six minutes. Spray the cones with a nontoxic silver-, copper-, or gold-colored paint.

Another place to find goods is at flea markets, swap meets, and garage sales. Check each basket's construction before making a purchase. You'll find many items at these places to use as gifts and enhancements. Proceed slowly and be careful not to overpurchase. Select only the items you truly believe will go into your baskets.

Supermarkets, gourmet shops, and candy stores sell delicious snacks and goods that will fill baskets. Supermarkets also sell bamboo skewers in the gadgets aisle. Edibles are found in a variety of stores, including pharmacies, cosmetics stores, and discount chains.

Office supply stores (Staples and its counterparts) house transparent and double-coated tapes, and they occasionally place mugs and post-Christmas snacks on clearance tables. If you belong to a warehouse club such as Costco, Sam's, or BJ's, these stores also sell many gift-basket-friendly items.

Don't overlook the linen chains. Years ago my daughter worked at one such store. She brought home soups, vinegars, and cookies packaged in cute boxes, bottles, and jars, all less than $1.00 each. The soups were packaged in jars with flowered fabric tied with cord around the lid. These specialty items are perfect for gift baskets, and the price is often lower than wholesale.

Professional florists purchase silk flowers and supplies from floral wholesalers, which are located in cities nationwide. Although conflicting stories are told, some of these outlets will allow the general public to buy. Professional designers are card-carrying members of these companies who do not pay sales tax because they resell products to the public. If you are able to purchase supplies, you will pay sales tax, but the savings are enormous and so is the selection of baskets, silk flowers, picks, ribbons, balloons, and more.

One drawback is that some products are sold by the dozen, but if the cost is low, it may be worth buying. Consider how many gift basket designs those eleven other items can be used in. Check your yellow pages under "Floral Suppliers" or "Floral Wholesalers" to see if there's one in your area. Call and ask if individuals are able to buy merchandise. If you are given the green light, it's a trip that's worth your time.

Tip: When visiting a floral wholesaler, think and act like a professional. Don't announce to fellow shoppers that you're a crafty person and that this is your first visit. Professional florists will not appreciate knowing that you're invading their territory. Inspect the aisles of merchandise as though you're in a craft store. Make your selections, pay for the supplies, and leave with the satisfaction that you've found great items to create many designs.

Also visit dollar stores and off-price discounters, which sell many types of gifts and goodies. Look for pretty tote bags and mugs, which you'll learn to design in chapter 11. Don't overlook candles, fragrances, and frames—three more products that dollar stores stock until a new batch arrives, just in time to make more gift baskets.

Select a medium-sized basket with a handle . . .

. . . but not one with inner partitions.

It's easiest to work with a basket that's the same width from top to bottom . . .

. . . because a basket that's wider on top needs more products.

Chapter 3

PREPARING THE INNER BASKET
Two Simple Ways to Fill Your Container

Before designers assemble their creations, they must prepare the inner basket. This involves filling the basket or container with a base material to elevate the contents, so that they can be seen above the basket's rim. There are two options for filling a basket: (1) newspaper or packing paper *or* (2) floral foam and tissue paper.

The supplies you'll need are:

- One medium-sized basket with handle, any shape. The basket should have no partitions on the inside.
- Three ounces of shred, any type. Three handfuls is equivalent to three ounces.
- Approximately 2 feet of packing paper or four full sheets of newspaper.
- One floral foam brick and one sheet of tissue paper, any color.

Select a basket with the same width from the top to bottom. Baskets that are wider on top need more products to look full. Your basket should also be flat on the bottom so that it doesn't wobble when filled. Take a minute and place the basket on the floor. If it sits flat, you've chosen a good vessel. If not, select a sturdier one.

Tip: Choose a workspace floor of wood, marble, or other nonfabric surface. Shred has a tendency to migrate downward and is easily removed by sweeping or vacuuming an uncovered floor.

OPTION 1: NEWSPAPER OR PACKING PAPER

Set your basket on a sturdy table or horizontal workspace. If the basket is made with a tight weave (the slats are against each other), then you can proceed to fill it with paper. If the basket contains an open weave, however, it must be lined with tissue before the paper is added. This will keep the newspaper or packing paper from being seen through the slats, which detracts from the presentation.

1. Line an open-weave basket with tissue before filling it.

2. The tissue should prevent newspaper or packing paper from peeking through.

3. Add crumpled paper to the basket.

4. Press the paper down firmly with your fist.

5. Continue adding paper to about 1 inch from the basket's rim.

6. Topping the basket with shred hides the paper from view.

7. Shred has a will of its own!

Crumple one sheet of newspaper within your hands, and insert the wadded paper into the basket. For packing paper, use a piece approximately 25 inches in length. Continue to crumple additional paper, and insert it until the bottom of the basket is covered. Use your fist to press the paper firmly downward into the basket. Do not be gentle; you are building a tight foundation so that the contents will stay in place and above the rim rather than sink down into the basket.

Continue to add crumpled paper on the inside until there is approximately 1 inch of empty space between the top of the paper and the basket's rim. Make sure the paper is tightly packed. Have additional paper available in case you need more.

Add an even amount of shred on top of the paper. The shred should be even with or slightly above the basket's rim. When finished, you should not be able to see any paper on the inside. Shred that falls over the rim is acceptable. It's a material that cannot be tamed, so let it hang.

OPTION 2: FLORAL FOAM AND TISSUE PAPER

Floral foam is approximately 9 inches long, 4 inches wide, and 3 inches deep. In most (but not all) cases, it will have to be cut or trimmed to fit the basket's cavity.

Place the foam on top of the basket to determine how much should be cut. This is best done by estimation, though you can mark the foam using a pen or pencil for support. Put the foam on the table and begin cutting it into shape. Be careful not to cut too much at one time. Return the foam to the basket. If it fits, you're ready to cover it with tissue paper. If not, continue trimming until it sits comfortably inside the basket.

Tip: For large or oversized baskets, fasten two foam bricks together using U-shaped pins. Place the two bricks together where joining will occur, and insert a pin's ends into each brick. Put one pin in the middle, or place two pins about one inch apart, including a pin on the opposite side if needed.

Because of the basket's depth, the foam might be positioned well below the rim. This is remedied by adding paper to the basket's bottom as described in Option 1. The difference is that here you'll add a small amount of paper to raise the foam, rather than filling the entire basket with paper. Start with two crumpled pieces. Press each into place. Insert the foam to test its height. When the foam is even with the rim, you're ready to proceed.

1. *Floral foam makes an excellent basket-filling alternative.*

2. *You'll probably need to trim the foam to fit your vessel.*

3. Cut the foam a little at a time. You can always trim more later.

4. Keep trimming until the foam sits comfortably inside the basket.

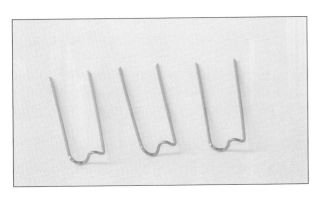

5. U-shaped pins let you join two foam bricks.

6. Insert one end of a pin into each brick.

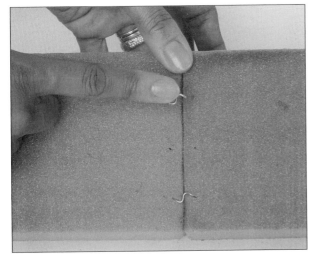

7. You can use more than one pin if needed.

8. Adjust the foam's height by adding wadded paper at the bottom of the basket.

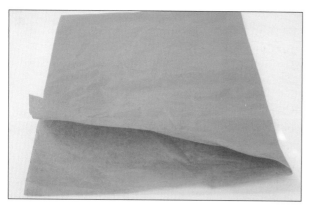

9. Fold a piece of tissue in half.

10. Place the foam brick facedown on the tissue.

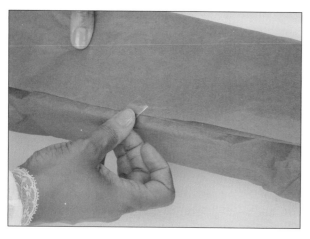

11. Enclose the brick in paper, closing with transparent tape.

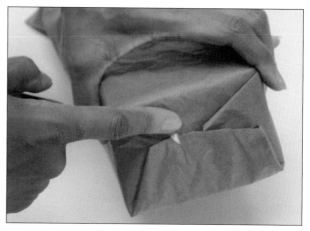

12. Wrap one end of the brick as you would a Christmas present.

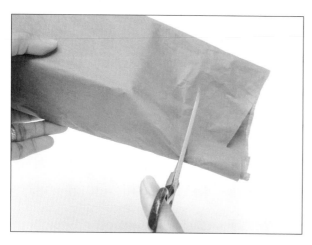

13. Trim excess tissue from the other end, then finish the same way.

14. Your covered foam brick should fit snugly in the basket.

15. Fill any empty spaces with shred. You're ready to make a gift basket.

Before the carved foam is inserted, it must be covered with tissue paper. Products will sit on top and should not do so on the exposed foam, which is gritty and unattractive. Even if you use a brick in a color other than gray (bricks are made in various colors), it should still be covered.

Fold the tissue paper in half. Place the brick in the middle of the tissue, with the top of the foam facing downward. (You can tell which side to put facedown based on how you trimmed the brick to sit inside the basket.) Wrap the tissue around the foam, and close it using one piece of transparent tape. Close one end of tissue and tape in place. Trim any excess tissue from the opposite end. Then close and tape it. Place the covered foam within the basket. The fit should be snug. Add shred to the basket in the gaps between it and the foam. Keep the top of the foam empty for now. It will soon hold snack and gift items.

WHICH METHOD SHOULD YOU CHOOSE?

Gift basket designers use both methods to fill the inner basket, according to their preference, skill level, and the types of products to be included. The foam-and-skewer method accommodates a basket with a heavy beverage bottle. A paper bottom works well for children's baskets, because skewers may prove dangerous to the recipient. Try both options to familiarize yourself with the techniques. Like the professionals, you may find yourself using one method for a certain design and a different method for the next.

BASKET FILLER DOS AND DON'TS

Over time you might encounter other filler options. Here are a few tips:

- *Do* substitute old cellophane for newspaper and packing paper. Cellophane is just as easy to crumple and this is an excellent way to recycle cellophane that's worn or dusty.
- *Don't* use Styrofoam peanuts as a basket filler. This product can be an unstable and undependable foundation material. Some professionals have mastered their designs using peanuts (as you'll learn in chapter 13), and you may do so in the future. For now, however, working with paper or foam and skewers is best.

Unless you know how to make products stand upright, your baskets will probably look like this!

Chapter 4

BASIC BUILDING TECHNIQUES

Proper Placement of Snacks and Gifts

If you've ever tried to make a gift basket without knowing how to make foods stand upright, the contents were probably tilted at a forty-five-degree angle. This chapter will teach you two methods to avoid this problem by properly anchoring your products. The first method uses the paper-filled basket and glue dots; the second involves attaching bamboo skewers to your snacks and inserting them into floral foam. These techniques correspond with chapter 3, where you learned how to fill your basket with either paper or floral foam.

For Option 1, you'll need:

- Basket filled with packing paper
- Snacks and/or gifts
- Glue dots

or for Option 2, assemble:

- Basket filled with tissue-covered floral foam
- Skewers
- Transparent tape
- Double-sided tape

The basket you select should be sized in proportion to the number of items you'll include. For example, a medium-sized basket, approximately 11 inches in diameter, will hold seven to eight items without looking sparse when complete.

OPTION 1: PAPER METHOD

This technique is for the basket that contains tightly packed paper topped with shred.

Group all the contents together on your tabletop or workspace. To design your basket, taller items will be placed in the back, graduating to the shortest items in front. This basket will include popcorn, two types of cookies, crackers, a turkey roll, cheese, jam, and water. These products are commonly used in basket themes such as birthday, thank-you, good luck, and congratulations. You can modify each arrangement by selecting ribbon and tissue

1. Assemble your gifts according to height.

2. To create a basket using the paper method, begin by making an opening in the shred with your hand.

3. Fill the opening with your tallest product—in this case, popcorn.

4. Tidy up each package as you insert it.

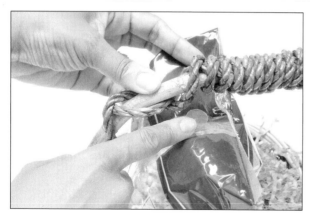

5. Adding a glue dot between popcorn and handle . . .

6. . . . will help hold the product upright.

7. *Continue adding products one by one, the taller in back . . .*

8. *. . . and the shorter in front.*

colors, embellishments, and product labels that denote the occasion. For example, a product labeled HAPPY BIRTHDAY would be added to a birthday basket, as shown for this design.

Each product will enter the basket at a specified insertion point within the shred and on top of the paper. The popcorn is the tallest item and will be added first. Use your hand to make an opening (hole) within the shred. This exposes the paper so that the popcorn will sit on top. Next, add the popcorn into the opening. Lightly press the popcorn down onto the paper, and lift the shred up and around the popcorn. About ¼ inch of shred will sit around each item after it is inserted. The popcorn now sits firmly in place. Look at the item, and fix the top of the package to remove any crumpled edges. This type of bottom-to-top inspection is required for each product.

Tip: Not all products have to face forward. Some items can face sideways or backward. It's your design. Experiment!

Contents often need support to stand tall or up against each other. For example, the popcorn may tilt toward the front. This is a temporary situation; it will stand straight as other products are added. If your basket's handle is positioned from front to back, you can place a glue dot between the back of the popcorn's packaging and the inside of the handle. Once done, the popcorn should stand tall on its own until the receiver removes the bag.

Continue adding each product, working with taller items in back and shorter ones in front. Glue dots can be placed between products that need extra support.

Keep All Labels Visible

Once your products are positioned, you need to assess whether the placement is really working. For instance, shorter items shouldn't be buried so deep within the shred that the receiver (and you) cannot see their names. An example of this is the jar of jam (shown below).

Rather than hiding it, elevate the jar by first removing the item, then adding a small amount of extra paper on top of the packed paper. Press the new paper down firmly. Put the product back in place, and add shred around it. The design is correct if you can see all or part of the product's name.

Fact: Every product name won't be fully exposed, because many package labels place the product name in the middle of the packaging, where it may disappear in back of the shred or behind another closely placed item.

However, step back and take a look at the completed design. If you can't see a portion of each product's name, elevate and reposition the products.

1. *Problem: The jar of jam is set so deeply here that its label is hidden.*

2. *Solution: Remove the jam and add a bit more wadded paper, pressing down firmly.*

3. *Return the jar to the basket, touching up with shred.*

4. *Now the jam is clearly visible.*

5. *Step back and inspect your finished basket. Can you see all or part of each product's name?*

OPTION 2: SKEWER METHOD

Gift basket designers in all stages—beginners, intermediates, and experts—use the skewering method. This is especially true when securing a large bottled beverage or something similarly heavy. For this design, we will use the basket with tissue-covered floral foam.

Select the products that will be added to the basket, and place them on the tabletop along with five skewers. Each product will be placed within the basket using the same method as for the nonskewered design: tall in back, short in front. The first item, popcorn, will not need a skewer, because the opening between the basket and foam is large enough to fit the bag. Remove some of the shred within the opening, and then carefully push the popcorn down into place.

The next step is to add a skewer to the cookie box. Break a skewer into three pieces, setting two of them aside. Determine where the skewer will be taped onto the box. In this example, the skewer will be taped in back. Using your thumb, hold one-third of the skewer against the box. The rest hangs below. Cut a piece of transparent tape long enough to cover the skewer resting against the box. Place the tape directly on top of the skewer.

Cut a piece of double-coated tape to exactly the same size as the transparent tape. Put the double-coated tape directly on top of the transparent tape (on the box). Now grab a fingerful of shred, and press it against the double-coated tape. This technique masks the skewer and will blend into the shred to be added later. Hold the cookies, placing your thumb on top of the covered skewer. Gently bring the box down onto the foam, piercing the tissue with the skewer as it is inserted. To keep the cookies from twisting, secure the box with a piece of transparent tape and place it evenly between the box and the foam.

Tip: Reposition the product on top of the foam if it's crooked or not properly set. Do this as many times as needed until you are satisfied with the placement.

Continue to add products within the basket using the skewering technique. As with the popcorn, you may find that some products fit snugly in the openings between the foam and basket. When completed, add shred to hide the tissue-covered foam. Look closely, and fill in all gaps. Inspect your design to ensure that the tissue and skewers are masked.

This basket looks exactly like the packed paper basket. Because of your masking techniques, you'd never know that skewers were added. Your gorgeous design is ready for enhancements.

1. To assemble a basket using the skewer method, begin by placing the tallest product between basket and foam.

2. Break a skewer into three pieces.

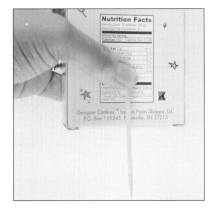

3. Hold one-third of the skewer piece against the cookie box using your thumb. Tape the skewer into place.

4. Cover the transparent tape with double-sided tape.

5. Press the shred into the two-sided tape so that the skewer is hidden from view.

6. Gently insert the skewer into your foam brick.

7. To keep the cookies firmly in place, add a piece of tape between box and foam.

8. Complete the assembly by adding shred as needed. Your basket is ready for embellishments.

Pull together your basket's theme with a multitude of embellishments.

Ting-ting is popular with basket makers.

Shorten ting-ting's stems with wire cutters or with your hands.

If your basket is packed with wadded paper, use shears to create a hole for embellishments.

Chapter 5

FINISHING TOUCHES
Choosing Enhancements That Bring
Your Design Together

There are many beautiful products out there that can add dazzle to your baskets and pull the theme together. If you are making a birthday basket, you might choose frosted balloons, star spray, and a festive pick. For a new baby, pink or blue embellishments are the best choices.

Other ideas are:

- Onion grass
- Star spray
- Flags
- Birds
- Flowers
- Ivy and other greenery
- Many other products that you'll find at craft shops

There's also twisted tamboo grass, which is known by the nickname "ting-ting." It's a product made from thin strands of wood that are straight at the bottom and curled at the top. Each strand is heavily coated with a sparkly substance in gold, silver, blue, red, and other colors. Ting-ting is tall, so you'll need to shorten the stems using wire cutters, or break it apart with your hands before adding it. Be careful if you're breaking the stems between your fingers, because these artificial fibers are splintery and can become embedded in your skin.

Tip: The best time to buy enhancements is at the end of a season, when craft stores lower their prices. For example, spring picks go on sale in late June. You can save 50 percent or more, and many picks are usable until early fall. Poinsettia picks go on sale days before the Christmas holiday. Buy at the last minute if you can wait. If not, buy these picks after the holidays and save them for next year's baskets.

You may encounter difficulty adding enhancements to a paper-packed basket due to the stems' inability to pierce the paper. Use your scissors or another sharp object to make a hole in the paper. If needed, temporarily remove the shred in the area to access the paper. Then insert your enhancement. Deepen the hole if necessary and repeat the process.

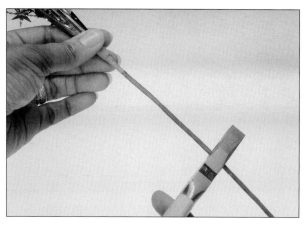

You'll need wire cutters to shorten some enhancements.

Use scissors to curl bits of star spray for an interesting effect.

You can also wrap star spray around your finger to create curls.

Insert star spray into the hole you created with your scissors.

Medium-height enhancements can be added to a basket's sides.

Diminutive picks look great in front.

The three enhancements in this basket—star spray, medium pick, and short pick—look terrific together.

If your enhancement towers over the tallest part of the basket, shorten the stem with wire cutters. This star spray embellishment is purchased tall and straight. Add character to it by carefully curling the grassy pieces with the open blade of your scissors. Curl the wired stars around your finger, and then gently pull the stars up for elevation. Now you can add the star spray to the design within the hole created by your scissors.

Inserting enhancements is easier in a floral foam-filled basket. As with skewers, stems pierce through the foam, allowing the enhancement to stand upright. Repositioning embellishments in foam is a simple process: Just pull the pick up and out and reinsert it wherever it looks more attractive.

Place tall enhancements, such as tingting and star spray, in the back and sides of your design. Medium-sized picks look great on the side, and short picks should be placed in front. Try not to overwhelm your design with assorted embellishments. Too many items can make your basket look busy and overshadow the

Wrap the wire ends of swag around the basket's handles.

Position the swag around the rim.

Grapevines can be tucked or pinned into place.

Complete your basket's look by adjusting the embellishments. Fan out the wired parts.

Your basket is ready to be wrapped.

around the basket's handle. Swags and grapes, two more popular embellishments, are often positioned around the basket's rim. Swags contain wired ends, which are bent and secured around the handle directly where the basket and handle intersect. Grapevines are soft and should be tucked between the inside basket and packed paper. If your basket contains floral foam, secure the grapevine's ends with U-shaped pins. The prongs are inserted into the foam, holding the vines in place.

Picks with wired parts, such as the medium pick of glittered berries and leaves added on the left side, contain branches that can be fanned out between, around, and above the contents. Now the basket is ready to be wrapped.

Tip: Try not to be overly critical when placing enhancements. Most new designers believe that their work is not up to par with other baskets. We've all felt that way, and it's just a matter of time before you begin to see the beauty in your work. Finish the design, add the picks, and walk away for thirty minutes. Then return and inspect the basket. It probably looks better than when you left the room.

wonderful snacks and gifts. This basket includes three enhancements and looks terrific.

Tip: Ting-ting is another embellishment that serves as a short pick. Break the long stems, leaving 2 inches on the bottom. Add the shortened ting-ting to the front of your design.

Ivy can be wound from end to end

Cellophane is a great basket-closing choice for beginners and is available printed or clear.

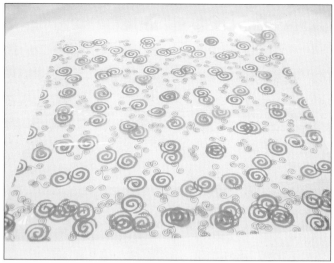

Basket bags are growing in popularity and are easy to use.

Shrink wrapping is a little more costly but creates the most professional-looking baskets.

Chapter 6

CLOSING THE BASKET

Proper Wrapping for a Professional Look

Essentially there are three basic methods for closing baskets that you'll need to consider. They include: (1) cellophane closure, (2) basket bag closure, and (3) shrink wrap closure. All three methods produce fine results.

Each designer should choose a basket-closing method by weighing the following factors:

- *Budget.* What supplies can you afford to purchase at present?
- *Ease of use.* You'll need dexterity to work with a shrink wrap machine and heat gun.
- *Expertise.* Extensive experience equals more money invested for supplies.

Most new designers learn how to close their baskets using cellophane because it's the easiest and most readily available product at a low price. Basket bags have grown in popularity and are considered easier to use than cello. However, it can be difficult to find bags when you begin designing.

Shrink wrap is the most costly invest-ment, requiring a shrink wrap roll or shells, shrink-wrapping machine, and heat gun. These products can cost $300 and up but can be found at a lower price through dis-counters. There's also a way to shrink your wrap without a machine, which I'll explain later.

All three closing techniques are widely accepted. Simply decide on a product to close your baskets and get started. Over time, you will either grow comfortable with that particular method and stick with it or decide to try others.

For this final basket-making step, you'll need:

- Cellophane *or* basket bag *or* shrink wrap roll or shell
- Heat gun or hair dryer (if using shrink wrap)
- Transparent tape
- Curling ribbon
- Bow
- Embellishment (optional)

Let's take a closer look at the many ways you can wrap your baskets.

CELLOPHANE CLOSURE

Cellophane rolls are made from plastic and can be purchased clear or printed. The most common cellophane roll is 30 inches wide by 100 inches long. This size is adequate for most baskets. However, cellophane rolls are also available 20 and 40 inches wide, which accommodate small and extra-large baskets, respectively.

To begin closing a basket with cellophane, roll the cellophane onto the table. Make sure that you roll it out in the underneath position, not overhand. This will ensure that the right side of the cello faces outward on your design.

Sit the basket on top of the rolled-out cellophane. Bring the front end up from the table. Extend it toward the ceiling, above the highest point of the basket. This end should cover the basket's front plus extend above the basket by about 10 inches. Increase the amount of cello to satisfy this requirement. Bring the roll of cello up the back in the same manner as the front side. Cut the cellophane, and set the roll aside.

Before closing the cellophane around the basket, measure it to ensure that the cello is even on the top and sides of the basket. Then return to holding both long pieces of cellophane at the top (around the basket's front and back).

With the front of the design facing you, bring the right side's edges together at the top and hold in place with your left hand. Working with your right hand, bring the cello lying flat on the table (the piece that connects the front to the back) up and parallel with the side of the basket. The cello's shape on the side now resembles a W or two Vs. In other words, one V of cello is in front of your wrist, and another V of cello is in back of your fingertips.

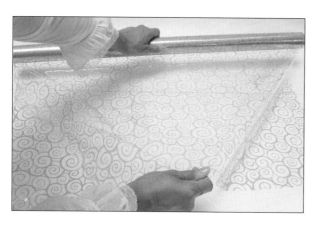

1. *To wrap your basket in cellophane, begin by rolling cello onto your work surface.*

2. *Unrolling from beneath ensures that the right side of the cello will face outward.*

3. Place your basket on the cello and extend the material up around the front.

4. Bring the cello roll up around the back of the basket as well.

5. Cut the cellophane about 10 inches above the basket's highest point.

6. Be sure there's an even amount of cello on the basket's top and sides.

7. Bring the right sides of the cello together at the top and hold.

8. At the bottom, lift the cello up parallel with the basket's side. The cello is now roughly W-shaped.

9. Fold the cello behind your fingers toward the front.

10. Now fold the remaining cello toward the back.

11. The cello should resemble a triangle.

12. Secure the cello with a piece of transparent tape.

13. Repeat the process on the other side.

14. After taping, the cello should completely cover the basket.

15. Next gather the cello atop the basket into one hand.

16. With your other hand pull the cello up to tighten.

17. Position the bow to face the front of the basket.

18. Tie the two ends of ribbon into a knot in back.

19. Use transparent tape to fix any gaps in the cello.

20. To fix uneven cello above the bow, gather it between your fingers.

Fold the cello behind your fingertips toward the front. Then fold the remaining cello (formerly in front of your wrist) toward the back. The cello should resemble a triangle. Let go of the cellophane above the design (in your left hand) and secure the triangle-shaped cello with transparent tape. If needed, place a second piece of transparent tape 1 inch above. You need a second taping if the cellophane comes apart when your hands are removed. Repeat this process on the opposite side. Make sure that the last piece of folded cellophane points toward the back of the basket. This will give your design a polished, professional look.

Next, gather the cellophane atop the basket into one hand. With the other hand, pull the cellophane upward from end to end (front and back) to give the plastic film a clear appearance around the basket. Pick up the bow and position it to face the front of the basket, where your hands are gathered around the cellophane. Bring the curling ribbon strings around on each side of the cello (around either side of your hand) toward the back, and tie tightly into a knot. If desired, add more curling ribbon around the neck, and curl the long ends with scissors. You can also use a ribbon shredder to cut the ends into curly shreds (an example is shown with the basket bag; see page 50).

Fix any cellophane gaps that appear around the bottom of the basket by placing transparent tape on a gap, then pulling down and taping underneath. Do this wherever gaps appear. Finally, fix uneven cello above the bow by gathering the cello between your index fingers and thumbs. Cut the cello in a fan shape. Your basket is now ready for presentation.

22. Voilà! Your gift is ready for giving.

21. Cut the cello into a fan shape.

BASKET BAG CLOSURE

Using a basket bag to close a design is said to be quicker and easier than using cellophane. For that reason alone, some designers prefer it. The bag is fused on three sides with an open end on top for easy basket insertion. The trick is selecting the right size bag for your basket.

A bag measuring 32 inches in height by 18 inches in width is a standard size that encases most medium-sized baskets. Measure your basket to determine the correct size bag. The chosen bag for your design should be 2 to 3 inches wider than the basket and at least 6 inches taller. This will give you just enough wiggle room to achieve a proper fit.

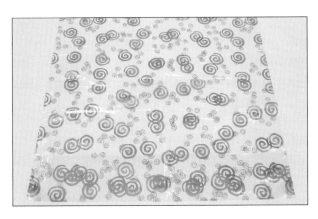

1. Many designers consider basket bags even easier to use than cellophane.

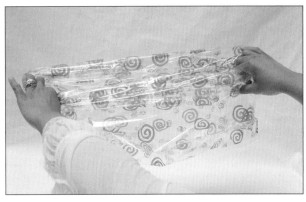

2. To use a bag, begin gathering the material together from the top until you reach the bottom.

3. Use your fingers to spread the bag open on your work surface.

4. Place the basket in the bag.

5. Carefully draw the bag upward until the basket is fully enclosed.

6. Now gather the bag at the top.

7. Smooth the bag by pulling upward.

8. Tie the bow into place.

9. If you like, embellish with extra ribbon.

10. Here, a ribbon shredder is used to curl the ribbon.

11. A pair of scissors will also give you this curly effect.

12. Double-check your bag for looseness after the bow is in place.

Starting at the top (open end), gather the bag together on both sides until you reach the bottom (fused bottom). Set the bag on the table, and place your index fingers and thumbs inside to open it widely. Set the basket inside the bag, then gently pull the bag up and over the basket. Be careful not to displace any of the basket's contents as you lift the bag upward. Once the bag has completely surrounded the basket, gather the bag together at the top. This is the same technique you used to close the cellophane wrapping.

Pull the bag upward to smooth the film around the design. When you're satisfied, add the bow around the neck and tie it into place. Add extra curling ribbon around the neck, and curl it with scissors or a ribbon shredder.

Tip: Cellophane can still be pulled upward for a clear appearance, even after tying the bow and curling ribbon around it. This is important if the cellophane seems to

be loose around the design. To check your bag for looseness, tug the cellophane at the top. Any additional looseness can be remedied by taping the cellophane down and under the basket.

Choose one of the two methods shown on page 52 to smooth any bottom gaps:

• **The single-fold method:** Fold the bag back (in one fold) to the side, and tape it into place. Fold the excess underneath the basket and tape. Use tape to eliminate any leftover gaps. Finally, pull the tape downward, and secure.

• **The multifold method:** Fold the bag in ½-inch folds toward the back of the basket until the bag is parallel with the side. Fold the excess bag underneath the basket and tape into place using transparent tape. A small piece of tape might be needed on the side of the bag to secure the folds. Use tape to eliminate additional gaps around the bottom edges.

Your bagged basket is complete.

The single-fold method:

1. *To narrow any gaps in the bottom, you can fold the bag to the side and apply tape.*

2. *Then tape any excess bag material beneath the basket. Pull the tape downward and secure.*

The multifold method:

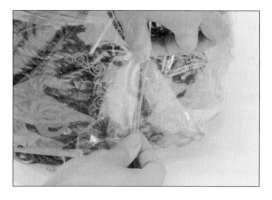 

1. *Another way to narrow any gaps is to fold the bag material toward the back of the basket in many small folds.*

2. *Fold the excess beneath the basket and secure with tape.*

Your design is complete. The bagged basket is ready for delivery.

SHRINK WRAP CLOSURE

Photographs in chapter 2 have introduced you to the dynamic duo—the shrink wrap machine and heat gun. You also learned, however, that these aren't the only tools that will allow you to shrink-wrap your gift baskets. Craft stores also sell shrink wrap shells, which are bags with rounded top corners. And you can find shrink wrap on rolls that resemble cellophane but are clearly marked for use with a heat gun.

Shrink wrap machines are used by professionals who've invested in such a machine because they employ it repeatedly. You can also add a shrink-wrapped look to your baskets at a fraction of the cost by purchasing a roll or shell. Here's how to use both.

Shrink Wrap Roll

Open the roll onto the table much as you would cellophane. Place your finished basket on top of the shrink, bringing the material evenly around the front and back of the basket. Add 10 inches above the tallest point in the basket. Cut the shrink wrap, and set the roll aside. Remove the basket from atop the shrink wrap. Cut a long piece of curling ribbon (about arm's length), and place it to the side.

Upon closer inspection, you'll notice that the shrink wrap is doubled. One long side is a center seam, while the other side is unfused (open). Open the shrink wrap, undoubling it to become one large piece. Place the basket in the middle of the open wrap, and bring the shrink wrap evenly around the basket. Hold the shrink in one hand, and pull it upward toward the ceiling to give the wrapping a smooth appearance around the basket. Remove your hand while tying the curling ribbon around the gathered shrink wrap to keep it in place.

Place your heat gun or hair dryer on the highest setting, and begin shrinking the film on the bottom. Turn the basket by hand,

1. *Open a roll of shrink wrap much as you would cellophane.*

2. *Enclose the basket in shrink wrap, extending it about 10 inches over the top.*

3. *Cut the wrap. Remove the basket from the wrap and set it aside.*

4. *A close examination will reveal that shrink wrap is actually doubled.*

5. *Open your piece of shrink wrap, place the basket atop it once again, and bring the wrap evenly up around it.*

6. *Pull upward to smooth the shrink wrap.*

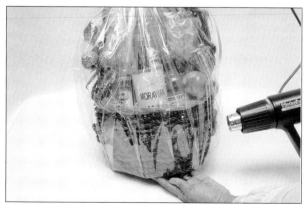

7. *Tie a ribbon around the gathered shrink wrap.*

8. *Use a heat gun or hair dryer to shrink the film. Start from the bottom, and continue up the basket with even strokes.*

9. Strive to make the wrap as tight as possible.

10. Put the finishing touches on your basket by adding a bow.

11. Trim the top.

12. Your gift is complete.

using even strokes on the front, sides, and back. Don't keep the heat gun in one place too long, or you'll risk tearing the film to expose a hole in the shrink wrap.

Gradually move upward to shrink the wrap, working steadily to make the wrap as tight as possible. Shrink wrap from a roll doesn't tighten as much as a shell, but it presents a good appearance when you're on a budget. Avoid shrinking the wrap above the curling ribbon. Before fin-

ishing, review your work and fix any unshrunk areas. Add a bow on top, and trim the shrink wrap above the curling ribbon. Your design is complete.

Tip: Take your time working with shrink wrap. The first few times you use a heat gun, you may end up with an uneven appearance or torn shrink around the basket. This is normal and will happen less often as you continue to practice with these materials.

Shrink Wrap Shell

A shell contains a fused top with rounded corners and an open bottom. Open the bag using your fingers and bring the open shell downward around the basket. Pick up the basket, and fold the excess shell underneath. Place two short pieces of transparent tape onto the opposite direction of the fold (across the shell) to close the excess neatly under the basket, and set the basket onto the table. There's no need to completely seal the shell with tape because the heat gun will seal the wrap.

Tip: Purchase a shell that's as close as possible to the size of your basket. This will ensure that there's no excess shrink material, which leaves an unsightly appearance.

Begin shrinking the shell with your heat gun, starting on the bottom. Gradually work upward, saving the wide sides for last. Hold the extra wrap on one side outward with your hand, and shrink this area gradually until it's tight. Repeat on the opposite side. Inspect your work, and shrink the wrap on the underside of the basket before turning off the heat gun.

Use your scissors or the sharp end of a bamboo skewer to punch a small hole in the front and back of the shrink wrap where a bow will be placed. Carefully thread the bow's curling ribbon through the hole, and tie into place. You can also add a self-stick bow, which does not require a hole in the shrink wrap. Self-stick bows, which are also sold in craft stores, contain a peel-off paper that reveals a sticky substance. Simply peel off the paper and press it onto the shrink wrap.

Your shrink-wrapped gift basket is complete.

1. To use a shrink wrap shell, begin by working the shell downward around your basket.

2. Fold any excess shell material beneath the basket. Secure with tape.

3. Set the basket on your work surface for shrinking.

4. Carefully work your heat gun around the basket, beginning at the bottom.

5. Work your way upward.

6. Hold the extra wrap outward on each side and shrink until tight.

7. Use shears or a skewer to punch a hole in the shrink wrap for a bow.

8. Tie the bow into place.

9. *Shrink-wrapped gift baskets have a sleek, professional appearance.*

ONE LAST LOOK AT FINISHING TOUCHES

Designers often add embellishments to the top of a design to add color and extend the height. You can achieve the same ends by inserting star spray or balloons into the top of your cellophane or basket bag. Watch the stem of the star spray as it is inserted so that it does not puncture a product's packaging when lowered.

Holes in your shrink wrap caused by excessive heat can be masked by adding an embellishment. Trim the wired stem, if necessary, before insertion. Then bring the enhancement into the hole. Fan out any leaves on your pick. Add glue dots between the leaves and shrink wrap for added support. Note that the berry pick and leaves shown below hide any wrapping errors.

Your wrapped basket can be decorated with embellishments to add height . . .

. . . or to cleverly conceal wrapping errors.

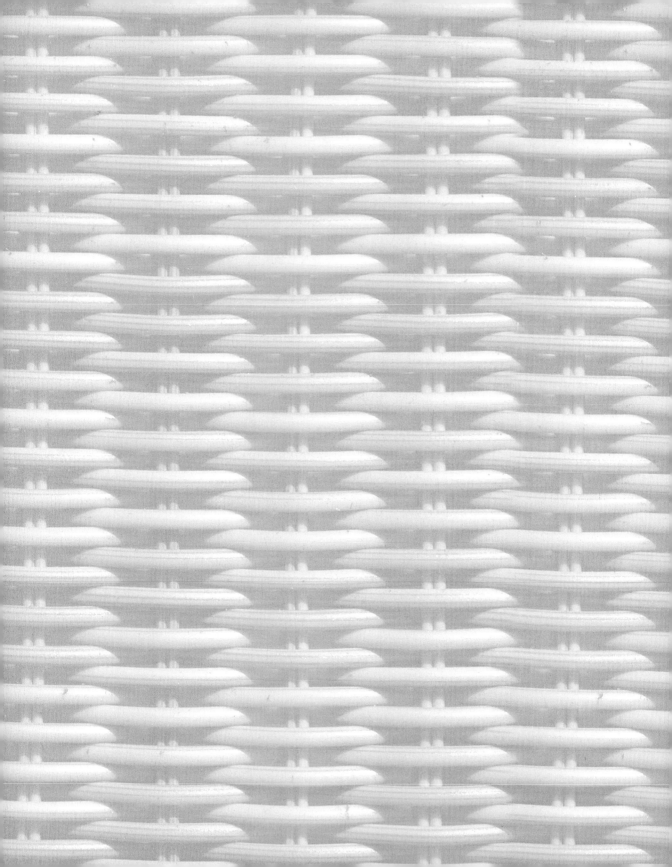

PART TWO
Baskets for Different Occasions

The Happy Birthday basket.

Choose birthday-themed gifts and snacks as well as products selected especially for the recipient.

In this basket the popcorn can face either forward or backward. Here it's turned to the front.

Transparent tape helps support the products.

Chapter 7
POPULAR OCCASIONS
Making Memorable Everyday Baskets

Each day, gift baskets are made and presented to people all over the world. The five designs shown in this chapter represent the most popular reasons for giving, as proven by statistics gathered from designers worldwide. You'll also find yourself making these baskets often.

HAPPY BIRTHDAY

There is no occasion more popular for gift basket giving than a birthday celebration. The basis for a terrific birthday basket is to know what types of snacks and gifts the recipient prefers. Does he like to cook? Then mixes and utensils create a satisfying gift. Does she love snacks with various flavors? That's what you choose. Also consider incorporating the person's favorite colors and gifts.

This birthday basket highlights a green, orange, and yellow color scheme. It uses a short, green-colored basket with brownish red trim along the top edge. The handle runs from side to side, but the basket could just as easily have been designed with a front-to-back handle. Green tissue paper lines this basket, topped with packing paper and orange-colored shred. Added to this birthday basket are cheese straws, cookies, corn snacks, peanut-butter-flavored popcorn, and a key ring that says NOT OLDER, BETTER. This basket was a good candidate for the floral-foam-and-skewers method, but the glue dots anchor the products in place so well that skewers aren't needed. Transparent tape was added from the back of the cookie box to the handle as extra support. Positioning the handle from side to side made this anchoring technique easier.

The cookie box with HAPPY BIRTHDAY written on it is stationed in the front so that the theme is obvious. If such a box is positioned at the back or other area where the birthday words aren't visible, a placard like the one in the Congratulations basket, which announces the theme, could be used instead (see page 66). The popcorn, which is placed at the back, faces forward

Embellishments—including a horn blower and a small pick—continue the birthday theme.

but could have been turned backward since it's the last product. However, the recipient can easily see the popcorn through the clear bag, which makes the forward positioning acceptable.

Birthday baskets can be filled with snacks and gifts or might encompass the wishes and desires of a person who seeks to create a change in life over the next twelve months. For example, if the person wants to start a business or already has an office, this basket might include any of the following: a business start-up book, name-engraved writing instrument, paperweight, business card holder, note cube, motivational calendar, car mileage logbook, desk nameplate, candy jar (with individually wrapped candies), and prepaid phone card to cut the expense of initial telephone calls. An alternative container for this gift is a briefcase. You'll see how to use different types of containers in chapters 10 and 11.

A person who loves to sew might receive a compact sewing kit, sewing machine needles, several spools of thread, a gift certificate for new patterns or material, a tracing wheel, and a box of straight pins. A sewing box to hold these new items is a wonderful alternate birthday container.

Keep the recipient's dietary restrictions in mind. For example, my aunt cannot eat chocolate, so it shouldn't be added to her basket. Ask the receiver in a matter-of-fact tone about any allergies to foods, or check with the receiver's friends or family members to ensure that the basket you make is filled with items that can be eaten rather than given away.

Enhancements run the gamut, from frosted balloons to HAPPY BIRTHDAY announcement sticks (similar to the one shown in the New Year's basket—see page 88) to horn blowers and other noise-makers. This one incorporates a green star spray, a horn blower with green and yellow fringe, and a small orange and yellow pick, which supports the key ring. Because birthdays are such a joyous time, anything that puts a smile on the recipient's face is a gift contender. This includes items that are nostalgic, trendy, or eclectic, or anything that makes a fashion statement. Local craft and discount stores sell many items that will help you create a birthday basket the recipient will long remember.

The Congratulations basket.

Tissue paper lines the basket to make sure no filler shows through its open weave.

CONGRATULATIONS

An individual receives a promotion, learns a baby is due, or hears some long-awaited good news. What a great time to offer congratulations! This magenta-colored basket lined with white shred contains a wide weave, so tissue is used on the inside to hide the mechanics. Floral foam and skewers anchor the contents and help keep the bottle in place so that it doesn't sink down into the basket.

Products in this basket are snicker-doodle-flavored coffee, fortune cookies, cheese straws, vineyard-themed pasta, and a wine sauce. These items are wide and weighty, which makes this large basket a terrific choice. There's no doubt about the reason for this basket. The fortune cookies are specifically for celebration, and a sign is placed on the left side announcing the theme.

Purple is a bright and vivid color, and is used in the content's packaging, sign, and star spray enhancement. The white shred between the basket and products makes the color more evident. Purple shred was another option, but it would have darkened the gift, whereas the bed of white shred makes the purple stand out beautifully. The two enhancements, a short pick and tall star spray, add balance and beauty to this design.

Notice the tissue showing between the basket's middle knots. Inspect your design to ensure that tissue is all that's visible around the entire basket. It may not be noticeable to the recipient, but it's an exas-

Ribbon helps keep the bottle of wine sauce securely in place.

perating feeling to notice newspaper or foam peeking through the slats. You'll have to pull the design apart to repair a problem you should have detected earlier.

The bottle of wine sauce, which complements the pasta, is anchored using the skewering technique. For a bottle of this size, you may find that attaching two 3-inch skewers, about 1 inch apart, keeps the bottle from twisting. To secure the bottle further, curling ribbon was tied and knotted around the bottle's neck, then tied to the basket's handle. A bottle does not have to stand straight when using this method. You know it's anchored properly when it shows limited movement.

Each piece of the vineyard pasta resembles a bunch of grapes. This and other shaped pasta make wonderful alternatives to the long-and-straight type we're all so familiar with. Other shapes available in specialty stores include sports team logos, holidays, houses, and dollar signs. Shaped pasta is nutritious and flavorful, and it makes a basket appear handpicked for the recipient.

Many products can be used to fit the congratulations category. Candy cigars, a silver-plated alphabet-block bank, an expectant parent's log- or guidebook, and coupons for diapers or a diaper service fit a new-baby theme. Writing pads, a dictionary, healthy snacks, a laundry bag, and a roll of quarters commemorate a college acceptance letter. The congratulations basket shown here might be given to a person who's been promoted or a couple who've finalized the paperwork on a real estate investment. What better way to celebrate the start of an empire?

A person who's just purchased a new car might be congratulated with sponges, cloths, a car wash kit, air fresheners, a steering wheel cover, and glass cleaner, all enclosed in a pail. What do you give to someone starting a new job? Consider sparkling cider (as shown in the Good Luck basket on page 70), a key ring with a success statement, a business card holder, and a frame to place the picture of a loved one on the new desk. Breath mints are another option, though you must be careful regarding who will receive the mints and the spirit in which they're given. Some will appreciate them, and others may find them offensive.

Be aware of the recipient's preferences, and your congratulations gift basket will be a deeply appreciated present.

The Thank-You basket.

Turning the basket reveals more gifts.

THANK-YOU

Who says gift baskets must be big to make an impression? A thank-you gift usually isn't large. It's something that shows appreciation for kindness, such as minding the dog or feeding a fish for the weekend, collecting the mail and newspapers while out of town, or baby-sitting or tutoring at the last minute.

Small baskets work well for this theme, unless the appreciation is for an entire family and a large basket is appropriate. The wicker cup shown here (see top left) creates a heartfelt gift that, when given, conveys complete gratitude to the recipient. The cup's inside diameter is 6 inches. Packing paper and ivory-colored shred sit atop tissue paper decorated with grapes, which lines the inner cup. Your tissue paper can be plain or printed; or you could opt not to line the cup with tissue, because the weave is tight and doesn't reveal the technique.

A few tokens of kindness are added: a Thanks a Million celebration cake, Colombian coffee, amaretto-flavored sugar, and a peach-flavored spoon. The cake takes about one minute to make in the microwave. It's mixed with water in its clear packaging and then topped with the accompanying frosting and sprinkles. The cake also contains a balloon and candle. The teaspoon peeks over the left side of the cake.

The coffee and flavored sugar are revealed when the recipient turns the basket toward the back. Since the two items cannot be seen in the front, it's best to turn them backward so the product names are clearly viewed. This type of design is common. Many designers turn products to the side or back so that the recipient has a 360-degree view of the goodies. The tissue paper that lines the basket is taller in the back and helps pull the design together. You can make the tissue taller in the front as well. Here it's lower, so that the cake's emblem is easily shown.

Two berry picks are used, one on each side of the basket. You'll notice that most designs in this book don't show this type of balancing. If enhancements complement each other in this manner, then go ahead and add them. A stem with three plain leaves is added above the cake and to the back of the coffee. This piece was separated from another enhancement and was about to be discarded, but it looks nice here.

Notice that there's no top handle attached to this cup. This means that each product must be supported in one of two ways. Either you should make sure that the diameter is small enough to hold products snugly within the shred, or you can add glue dots between products to keep each item in place until the entire gift is separated.

Like many of the baskets I'll show you, this one can be presented to a man or woman. Make substitutes as needed—say, tea or cocoa rather than coffee. Other ideas for the Thank-You basket include popcorn, nuts, a notepad preprinted with the person's name, and a plush toy. You may also find fake million-dollar bills while searching through dollar stores. This fun money is great for lining the basket (instead of tissue paper), or it can be rolled, tied in the middle with curling ribbon, and inserted the same way you'd add a pick.

You'll find another design that can also be used as a thank-you offering in chapter 11—a tote bag (see page 126). Either of these designs makes a terrific gift to show your appreciation for a job well done.

The Good-Luck basket.

Chocolates and corn snacks are secured together with transparent tape.

A wineglass is tied to the basket's handle with ribbon.

GOOD LUCK

Here's another theme that can be created with a small or large basket, depending on the recipient and whether the contents will be enjoyed individually or shared with friends and family members. The wine basket depicted here includes a tall handle. Because the basket's weave is exposed, it's wise to place a small amount of shred on the bottom to cushion the bottle. Sparkling cider is used in this basket, but any type of bubbly is appropriate.

Added to the back are corn snacks and a tin of chocolates. The bottle hoists both items into place within the top half of the basket. Transparent tape secures the two products together at the back. Tape is also placed from each product to the outside of the basket, right below the handle. Not all baskets will allow for this type of taping, but this one features a thin weave, making it tape-friendly. You can see that snack or gift items added to this design must be small and thin to share space with a tall bottle. Anything large will be too awkward to secure.

Any combination of biscotti, a two-cookie pack, sausage, cheese, or a slim package of crackers will fit in the back or sides of the basket and complement the cider. One East Coast company sells short-bread shaped to resemble horseshoes and nails—both terrific for this theme. Look for these items in specialty stores. A tote bag can be used as a good substitute if the depicted basket is not available. You'll see such a bag in chapter 11.

Inserting the top of the cider bottle inside the glass helps prevent breakage.

Mardi Gras beads tied whimsically around the basket add a personal touch. A gingham bow completes the design.

Curling ribbon is used to tie a wine-glass to the basket's handle. The glass's stem is tied first, then anchored to the handle. The position allows the top of the bottle to be inserted inside the glass, saving space and minimizing contact between the two objects. Because the

bottle is wrapped in paper, there is little reason for either item to break upon contact. Your design style may lead you to anchor the glass directly at the top of the handle, which is also an acceptable choice. The embellishment, at the top left, is woven through the basket's triangular openings. Leaves and stems are wrapped around the handle, which keeps the pick in place.

Green Mardi Gras–type beads are wound around the basket, threaded through the back, and tied on one side with curling ribbon. This is a freehand method the designer created on a whim. The curling ribbon can stay long or be cut to a shorter length. You'll come up with your own unique ways to tie beads and other embellishments. The final enhancement here is a gingham-checked pull bow positioned on the basket so that the bottle's label is clearly readable.

This basket's theme is a close relative of the congratulations gift, with slight variations. Good-luck wishes are offered before congratulations are extended. They're appropriate for people pursuing a quest— perhaps taking the bar exam or applying for a job that hundreds of others are applying for at the same time. The Good-Luck basket can also be presented in lieu of a congratulations gift. For example, a person who gets a new job is a candidate to receive a Good-Luck basket, but the theme can be relabeled to offer congratulations. This type of versatility is something designers practice every day.

The Get-Well basket.

Soups and teas are appropriate for the Get-Well basket.

Products are chosen to be soothing and cheerful.

GET WELL

Tea and soup are the order of the day when presenting the Get-Well basket. The sample gift shown here has been created in a bushel basket, reminiscent of the type of container you might find at a roadside fruit and vegetable stand. The yellow trim is bright and cheery, which makes it perfect for the theme.

This basket includes two types of soup, two types of cookies, tea, a book with tea recipes, and a honey-flavored spoon. One cookie's packaging, on the right side, includes the words GET WELL. It can't be seen, however, because the words are covered by the tea book. Still, a smile should come to the recipient's face when the cookies are revealed.

Chicken noodle soup is said to have medicinal qualities that heal a person quickly. This flavor is well known, but the brand isn't carried by supermarkets. Such a specialty should lift the receiver's spirits. She-crab soup is an alternative flavor that's popular in southern states. (The name bears no relation to a person's mood when under the weather!) The flavored spoon is made with sugar and used to sweeten tea. It dissolves into the hot beverage, leaving the spoon clean and ready for tea tasting.

This basket is packed with paper and vanilla-colored shred. Start by inserting the soup and cookies in back, which will help support the products in front. The flavored spoon was added last after the designer viewed the complete design and decided

A grapevine can embellish a basket intended for a man or a woman. It's attached here to the basket's handle.

where it should be placed. Floral foam and skewers would also work, as long as the basket is presented to an adult who will discard the skewers responsibly.

The enhancements were chosen for a man or woman. Most men aren't big flower lovers, so these colors are toned down and acceptable while still attracting women. Another consideration for a woman's design is to choose enhancements that match the basket's trim. Yellow daisies, for example, would pull the theme together. The hydrangea at the back has a long stem and is set in place by using scissors to make a narrow hole within the paper. If you have trouble keeping the stem upright, you can add a glue dot between the soup and the stem, or tape the flower's stem across the back of the soup.

One long grapevine is strung in front to add punch to the plain basket. It is attached at the rim around the silver handle. Find a point on the vine where it will grab the handle. Add an extra vine around the back if you choose.

Bushel baskets aren't the only vessel to consider for this gift. An old-fashioned doctor's bag would make a wonderful container, and so would a tea cup and saucer, shown in chapter 11 (see page 138). You can also add a small tea cup and saucer within a get-well gift, as shown in the Bereavement basket in chapter 8 (see page 86). If the receiver isn't a tea drinker, try coffee, cocoa, cappuccino, or juice as a substitute. Lozenges go a long way toward healing a scratchy throat. Does the person dislike soup? Perhaps instant oatmeal with a banana is a better choice. Remember to include what the recipient prefers, not what you wish to give. That's what makes a gift memorable.

Keep in mind that fruit can be added to any gift basket design. The best place to buy fruit is at a local grocery store or specialty market where you'll select the best-looking apples, oranges, pears, grapefruits, and bananas. Only buy as much fruit as you need for your design, which is usually no more than three of any type.

When adding fresh fruit, use a skewer to prick the cellophane at least three times after closing it around the basket. This will allow fresh air to enter the design and keep the fruit from ripening too fast. Then deliver your basket as quickly as possible so that the fruit doesn't spoil.

The Housewarming basket.

Chapter 8

SPECIAL THEMES

Expressive Designs for Good and Sad Times

Change occurs over time in the lives of family members and friends. This chapter provides gift basket ideas for five recurring events that you might not have considered when giving gifts in the past. Be it a happy occasion (the purchase of a new home, the birth of a baby, a wedding) or a time for comfort (everyday stress or a death), there are many opportunities for you to express your sentiments to family and friends through a customized gift basket.

HOUSEWARMING

Good friends, new neighbors, welcome wagons, and parents who are emptying their nests all have one thing in common. Each has a reason to give a housewarming gift basket to someone who's moving into a new home, apartment, town house, or condominium.

Housewarming baskets contain a collection of functional, trendy, and whimsical items for the recipient, all depending on

the new home's inhabitants. Singles, newlyweds, alternative-lifestyle couples, and traditional families with children will receive many of the same items, but there are optional products to add for each group. The basket might also include products for in-laws and pets if the family structure includes these extended members.

A flavorful rum cake, pasta shaped to resemble houses, key-lime-flavored cheese straws, wine jelly preserves, pretzels (hidden by the enhancements at the back), and key lime dip are combined to create the wonderful housewarming design shown on the facing page. The basket is tall and sturdy. It's filled with packing paper and ivory-colored shred. The basket's tight weave assures that the recipient won't see the construction method, and the blue, pink, and off-white color scheme makes it a welcome addition to any household.

A berry embellishment is added in front, and a wildflower pick and star spray stand tall in the back. You can tie a bow to the handle, as shown on the right. This dual-ribbon bow of orange gingham and

Specialty pastas and other snacks help establish the theme.

Other products that work well in this basket theme are cider, drinking glasses, movie coupons, popcorn (ready-to-eat or microwave), tortilla chips, salsa, pasta sauce, bread sticks, a wall plaque, utensils, stationery, kitchen magnets, key rings, mugs, the recipient's city or state official magazine, a bill organizer, a homeowner's journal (as shown in the Wedding basket; see page 84), and a coupon holder.

If you're adding drinking glasses, the stems can be tied onto the handle in the same manner as shown for the Good-Luck (page 70) and New Year's Day (page 90) baskets. Be sure to secure the two glasses by placing a glue dot between them. That will prevent friction, which might otherwise increase the likelihood of breakage.

Another charming treatment for this design is to use a basket shaped like a house. If you can find such a vessel, there's no need for products that state WELCOME HOME or HOME SWEET HOME. The container's shape will designate the theme. Box containers are also available with house designs stenciled on the front, which is another option. Or try using a dish drainer, umbrella stand, or mesh waste container. Men will appreciate a toolbox or food tray table as the container for their housewarming gift.

This basket's contents and alternatives highlight how many products are interchangeable according to the recipient's preferences. Keep this in mind to create a cozy Housewarming basket.

yellow organza enhances this attractive design and accentuates the picks' colors.

The Home Sweet Home pasta is the product that defines this basket's theme. It is easily removed and replaced with another product—a tall box of chocolates, for instance, or a large beverage bottle—to create a different theme. This gift can then be presented as a wedding present, given to a person who's just arrived home after traveling abroad, offered as comfort after a recent divorce, or created for someone who's coming home from an extended stay in the hospital. (In the latter case, be sure to consider the person's dietary restrictions when you select the products.)

Baby basket I. This whitewashed bootie is a darling container for baby gifts.

Choose from a multitude of products that welcome the newcomer to the world. Duck toys can be substituted for the frogs if the parents prefer.

BABY

Creating a basket to welcome a newborn is an exciting task, but it's also filled with challenges. There are many items that you will want to add to this design, so you must plan what to buy ahead of time, or the gift will be as big as a college graduate when you're finished! With this in mind, here's a look at two designs that welcome the new baby to the world and a variety of alternate products that stand alone or can be added within each basket.

The first design (Baby basket I) uses a large whitewashed bootie. It contains the book *Fatherhood,* by Bill Cosby, a pink bunny-shaped rattle, a hooded receiving blanket, a miniature congratulations book, a baby-bottle candle, a frog family for bath-time fun, and two silver-plated receptacles, one for the baby's first lock of hair and the other for the first tooth. The latter is a wonderful keepsake item, which is housed in a cherry wood and surrounded by white silk fabric. If the recipient favors duck-shaped tub toys, those can be added instead of the frogs.

The bootie is tall, so packing paper was the best choice as filler material. It's an appropriate container for a boy or girl. It's lined with yellow shred that's easily replaced with a different color. Tissue printed with rattles and other baby toys helps keep the packing paper from view through the basket's weave. The receiving blanket inside the basket could be used to line the bootie in the same manner as the tissue.

This charming memento is designed to hold a baby's lock of hair and first tooth.

Baby basket II. A carryall container is used to house gifts for both parents and baby.

Other items that might assist the new parents include nail clippers, hangers, diapers, a night-light, diaper wipes, a comb and brush, a teething ring, and a feeding dish with spoon. We remembered Dad with a copy of Bill Cosby's book, but don't overlook Mom. Think about books in the genre she likes best, new-mother magazines, lotions and other pampering items, and a tote bag to pack necessities in the coming months.

The bootie is one of many containers available for a baby gift. A large basket is another candidate, as is a diaper pail, bathing tub, child's wagon, stroller, or compact changing station, as used by the women who assembled a baby basket in 1913.

You can change the look of your gift by substituting a carryall container (Baby basket II). This basket, which is foam covered in blue gingham, is soft and round in shape. The inside contains an extra piece of material that's tacked onto all sides, creating four inner pockets to hold teething rings and small items. A ruffle, made with blue gingham, is added around the outside. There's also a fabric handle made with the same material attached on two sides that's long enough to sit inside of the basket when not in use. The basket's bottom contains batting inside the gingham, giving the carryall extra stability.

Packing paper is the basic filler for this type of design. Floral foam will also hold items steadily, but skewers may seem out of place for a baby gift. In addition, newspaper will soil the gingham material and

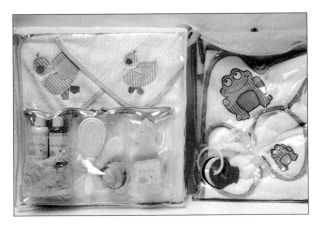

Baby gift packs make thoughtful basket additions.

A bunny-faced carryall makes another Baby basket option. More bunny products can be chosen to continue the theme.

the mother's hands as she removes it. This basket was made with a boy baby in mind, although the vanilla-colored shred can be exchanged for hot pink for a girl.

A receiving blanket, burp cloths, keepsake containers for first lock of hair and tooth, a lullaby CD, booties, and a plush animal welcome the newcomer to the

world. Green beads and a single green leaf are set on either side and bring balance to the design. Other products to consider are pacifiers, child protection locks, socks, bath wash, and lotion. Some of these items are shown here, such as pacifiers inside a large bottle that doubles as a bank. A pacifier and baby wash products are bundled within the two assembled gift packs. White, cushiony blankets trimmed in green or yellow stripes will keep the baby's skin soft. The yellow blanket is teamed with soap, lotion, shampoo, a brush, and tub toys. Either of these sets can act as a wall in back of a basket design, or other baby items can be stacked atop its flat surface to create a pyramid gift set similar to the Gourmet Tower shown on page 134.

There are other types of soft carryalls available, such as the example made from pink terry cloth and designed with a whimsical bunny face. Its round shape and deep opening will hold as many items as the blue gingham basket. A companion item for this holder is an ice pack covered in the same bunny shape used for teething (shown next to the carryall).

These baskets only scratch the surface of what's available for the new baby and new parents. Narrow your choices to include unique, yet practical items that the parents are less likely to receive from other gift givers. Team these with great containers such as the ones shown here, and you'll create a gift basket that will be treasured for a lifetime.

The Spa basket.

Decorative fans are easy to add.

Shorten the fans' stems with wire cutters. You can also snap them in half with your hands.

Insert a fan at the back of the basket.

SPA TREATMENT

Everyone loves to be pampered, including men. Who wouldn't want to receive a collection of exotic soaps, scrubs, and scents? Few will purchase it for themselves, however, which is why the spa basket is a popular gift for any occasion and gender. It can be given to say thank-you, as a stress reliever, for Mother's Day, or to a person who deserves a little downtime after a hectic event.

A small, country basket was used to create the contemporary design shown here. It's reminiscent of the days when folks soaked their cares away in wooden tubs, as seen in old Hollywood movies. Floral foam was carved to fit the basket and then covered in tissue before insertion. It's not easy to stabilize soaps, bath crystals, and lotion bottles in such a design, which is why floral foam and skewers were chosen.

Select products according to how the recipient prefers to be pampered. Some individuals love baths, while others head for the shower. Does the person have access to a spa, whirlpool, or sauna? If the recipient lives in a climate where sandals are the preferred foot gear, foot lotion will be appreciated. What about bath products that make lots of bubbles, and how about adding candles? Is the person allergic to certain fragrances? Think about all these options before deciding on what will create the ultimate pampering pleasure.

This petite basket holds soaps, lotions, spa crystals, body spray, hand and foot balm, eye cream, and candles. A jar of body cream sits below the spa crystals (at back right), giving it height above other products. Floral tissue paper envelops the inner basket around the floral foam. The tissue can be seen through the basket's openings. Star spray or ting-ting would make a nice presentation, but this design is limited to yellow pansies, which adorn the basket in front. Wrapping flowers around the basket's handle is another option.

One enhancement that's easily added is decorative fans. These fans are made from wood and sprayed with high-gloss or matte paint. As with other embellishments, fans are found at craft stores and a few discount shops. They're usually sold in bundles of six or twelve, but you might find a store that sells them individually.

First, choose two fans in a color that enhances your design, and that are similar in size and style. Each fan is made separately, so they are purchased in varied sizes. The stems are long and must be shortened with wire cutters. If wire cutters aren't available, grab one stem with both hands and snap it in half. Be sure to hold the stem away from your face to avoid injury. Repeat with the second fan. Try not to cut too much the first time, or the fans won't sit properly in the basket.

Insert the fan, stem-first, at an angle in back of the basket. Shorten the stem if the fan sits too high. Trim as needed beginning with 1-inch cuts until you're satisfied with the length. Reinsert the fan into one

Add the second fan at a complementary angle—or upright, depending on your design.

The fans create a dramatic and elegant backdrop for these pampering bath products.

side of the basket, and add the matching fan on the other. Some fans look better when they are upright rather than angled, depending on the design.

Look at the design. Do the fans enhance its appearance? Are the stems cut short enough that the fans do not over-power the design? This example shows how fans add an elegant "back wall." The fanless design is beautiful, but fans are a simple way to increase the gift's value, usually for just a few dollars. Which looks best to you?

When you think about spa baskets, you also dream of eating chocolates and drinking a bubbly beverage. While a bev-erage can be added, chocolates should never be tucked between soaps or scented products. Chocolates, in any form, will absorb the stronger scents and become unpalatable. Consider adding food items in another basket or simply presenting the snacks as an additional gift. Try this experi-ment if you insist on adding foods to a spa basket. Wrap the food in separate cello-phane, and then wrap the entire basket together. Wait a few days. Unwrap the basket, and taste the foods. If there's no trace of the scented items, you're cleared to present the same basket to another person. Designers nationwide play it safe by keeping foods away from spa products.

Other containers to consider for this design include miniature porcelain or plastic tubs, brass buckets, and tub caddies.

COMPLETED
Basket Designs

The Happy Birthday basket employs a cheerful green, orange, and yellow color scheme.

A purple-and-white color scheme gives the Congratulations basket an elegant look.

Even this tiny Thank-You basket makes a big impression on the recipient.

Sparkling cider in a wine basket along with a wineglass and a few snacks make up the Good Luck basket.

The Get-Well basket is a fruit basket full of soothing soups and teas.

Luxurious bath products are anchored in this Spa basket with floral foam and skewers.
A pair of fans completes the design.

The Housewarming basket is set in a tall, sturdy basket.

Orange gingham and yellow organza accentuate a Housewarming basket whose contents are both functional and fun.

The Baby basket (shown here in two versions) can be customized for either a girl . . .

. . . or a boy by changing shred and product colors.

A burgundy-colored table runner adds warmth and contrast to the whites of this Wedding basket. Scones, jams, chocolates, and candles are arranged in a picnic basket for the newlyweds.

A Bereavement basket needn't be large to extend condolences and comfort. Red, white, and green make a tasteful color scheme.

Drink glasses, healthy snacks, and breakfast items make up this New Year's basket.

Designed in the colors of the day, this Valentine's basket is embellished with a heart spray, flowers, a homemade bow, and punchinello ribbon.

What mother doesn't need a little help? That's where this wheelbarrow-shaped Mother's Day basket comes in, filled with products chosen especially for Mom.

The Father's Day basket is a study in open-and-eat snacks.

Star spray, a campaign hat, and red shred liven up this July 4 design.

The Thanksgiving box is so colorful and festive it needs no enhancements beyond orange shred.

Christmas is far and away the biggest gift-basket-giving day of the year. This Christmas basket is designed to be appropriate for a man or a woman.

Cloth, leather, rope, and beads form the vessel for this Kwanzaa basket. This basket incorporates African- and Caribbean-based products and colors.

The Fruit-Decorated box uses a beautiful, reusable container.

This colorful box says "thank-you" in many different languages.

The Black-and-White-Striped box makes a classic, elegant corporate or congratulatory gift.
Use shred to add color.

A white brocade hat box, pink picks, and pink shred complete the Chocoholic design.

A burgundy Fleur de Lis patterned bag, silver eyelash ribbon, and metallic star spray form the Tote bag.

A trunk makes a popular gift container. Here the theme is Thanks a Million, but you can be as creative as you like. Yard sales make a good source for trunks.

An upside-down box serves as the base for this vertical Gourmet Tower of treats.

The Latte Tower combines snacks and beverages with a cup and saucer.

Mugs make charming gift receptacles. You might choose one that's personalized (left) or frosted (right). Glue dots between the products hold everything securely.

Flora Brown's California Garden basket is a big hit with homeowners. A water hose serves as its base.

Award-winning designer Flora Brown has created the Garden Helper basket, a favorite among Realtors who purchase it in multiples for their clients.

Elaine Essary creates beautiful gift baskets with premium treats, primarily for corporate clients.

Lise Schleicher created her award-winning Puttin' on the Ritz basket by combining a tuxedo container, smoked salmon pâté, and a platinum-colored bow.

Marie Pessolano and Marian Donnelly designed this beautiful gift basket—a study in purple, green, and gold.

The Wedding basket.

WEDDING

One wedding has the ability to keep your hands immersed in shred for days. Not only will you make a basket for the bride and groom, but other members of the wedding party are candidates to receive bridal party baskets. That includes the bridesmaids, men's party, mothers of the bride and groom, and the wedding planner. Still, your creativity can make $100 gift certificates pale in comparison.

A picnic basket was chosen to create this lovely gift. Its large size will come in handy when the newlyweds decide to enjoy sandwiches, snacks, and a sparkling beverage on a warm afternoon or late summer's night. This basket contains a scone mix, nonalcoholic cider, a scented candle wrapped in tulle, embroidered toilet tissue, a homeowner's journal, cookies, white cheddar popcorn, wine jelly, four goblets, and red roasted pepper jam. Notice the placement of the burgundy-colored table runner draped in front of the basket. It helps break up the white color and adds warmth to the design.

As with most basket designs in this

In this Wedding basket, one goblet holds a tulle-wrapped candle . . .

. . . while another contains roasted red pepper jam.

Embroidered toilet tissue and a journal are suitable gifts for the bride and groom.

book, packing paper and shred form the bottom foundation. The linen table runner lies flat within the inner front wall of the basket and is doubled in the front. There are many products within this basket, but depending on the couple's preferences, others can either be added or substituted. For example, if the couple met while traveling, postcards and other items that remind them of their initial meeting add a sentimental touch. For couples who share a love for photography, photo frames and photographic cleaning supplies show your thoughtfulness. Consider what the couple have in common, and include it among the snacks and gifts.

This basket should be adorned with the bridal party's colors, so make sure you know the palette ahead of time. The colors can be highlighted within the shred, embellishments, cellophane closure (unless a clear wrap is used), and some of the products' packages. Such a basket can be presented to the bride during the bridal shower or to celebrate an anniversary.

The handle on the bottom of the basket (see page 83) loops around another handle on top, which secures the basket while carried. The four goblets are held in place by white ribbon strung across the four inside corners of the basket. Each goblet sits comfortably and can be filled with shred or a small product, unless you prefer to leave the glasses empty. The goblet on the left is a perfect fit for the scented candle wrapped in tulle. The

goblet on the right holds the jam. This use of space gives the basket a full appearance. Aside from the linen, only one embellishment is used, which can be seen on the right in the lid. Fewer enhancements make the products the focal point. However, your basket should be styled with the type of embellishments that add glamour and beauty, so include the type of flora and fauna that celebrate the day's union.

Embroidery, as shown on the toilet tissue, adds a touch of elegance to a product that's known more for its functionality. Consider the first letter of the couple's last name as an embroidered touch on something you add to a basket. The homeowner's journal is an item every couple should have to document valuables, mementos, and changes in their home over the years.

Smaller baskets for the bridal party might include personalized or engraved items, bubbles and a wand, lotions, foot soaks and sprays (to soothe their feet after the festivities), and a picture frame to hold the bridal party picture. The maid or matron of honor's basket can include the same items plus another special gift, and her basket should be created with a slightly different color scheme than the rest of the bridal party. Use special ribbon imprinted with a wedding wish or other sentiment to close these gifts after applying cellophane or shrink wrap.

This Bereavement basket is an asymmetrical design with a linen napkin on the right and shred on the left.

The cup and saucer are secured with a glue dot.

BEREAVEMENT

Gift baskets are associated with joyous events, but the Bereavement basket takes a detour from celebratory giving. This basket's mission is to bring comfort to one or more persons who've lost a loved one. Not only is it given when a close relative passes, but it is also becoming an accepted gift to offer when a pet departs. If you browse through greeting cards, you will notice that the pet card section is increasing in size. That's a strong indicator of how important gifts for grieving pet companions have become.

This beautifully tailored gift is contained in a small dark red basket filled with packing paper and ivory-colored shred. The rim is sprayed with a brushed gold paint. Much like the Thank-You basket (see page 68), this gift does not have to be large in size to convey the sentiment. Included are two coffees, tea, lemon curd mix, an apple-flavored spoon, a small cup and saucer, a gold-plated spoon, a picture frame, and a linen napkin. The embellishment tastefully incorporates delicate flowers and a butterfly.

Notice that the handle is positioned from front to back, whereas the birthday basket's handle (see page 64) is side to side. A glue dot is added between the cup and saucer, which keeps the pair from breaking due to pressure or rough handling while in transit. The linen napkin was added to the basket before the other items so that one side would sit flat along

Adding products to the back of a basket helps use space efficiently.

the basket's inner wall. Your napkin does not have to be angled in this position. Arrange it in a way that flatters the basket and its contents. Notice how shred is visible on the left side while being absent on the other due to the napkin's inclusion. It proves that a basket can look beautiful without symmetry.

The second coffee, a chocolate mint flavor, is not visible until you turn the basket backward and see the coffee directly behind the lemon curd mix. You don't have to place products in back, as done here, but it is a good use of space. The idea was simply to add another beverage option for the recipient. The primary color scheme (green, white, and red) also influenced the addition of a second coffee.

Frames are added to many bereavement baskets. During this grieving period, frames are not a priority to the recipient, but it will be considered a thoughtful ges-

ture to house a picture of the departed. A frame size of 3 by 5 or 4 by 6 inches is appropriate for a small or medium basket. Coffee and tea are known for their comforting qualities, but as with all designs, recipients should receive their preferred beverage. For the lemon curd mix, you might substitute a mix for scones or other breads. Shortbread or chocolate chip cookies, biscotti, lemon straws, a small cake, and individually wrapped hard candies are excellent options as well.

Many gift items, such as the frame and cup-and-saucer combination, are available for this basket. Cards and envelopes for thank-you notes, poem books, and flower seeds make thoughtful inclusions. While baskets are terrific vessels, also consider small multicolored boxes, such as shown in chapter 10, or a flower pot, especially if you're adding seeds.

If you plan to ship this gift to another state, be sure to wrap the tea cup and saucer individually in bubble wrap, which is available at any office supply store. The items can be reinserted into the basket after the protective wrapping is added. Frames should also be wrapped so the glass won't break. Shrink wrap is the preferred closure method for shipping. Often, however, designers use a double layer of cellophane around the gift in place of shrink wrap before packing it for shipping.

Bereavement baskets may not be a gift you'll make often, but each design created with your loving hands will soothe the receiver in the difficult days ahead.

The New Year's basket.

Chapter 9

CELEBRATING THE HOLIDAYS
Sharing Love, Laughter, and Tradition

Searching through malls to find the right gift for someone who has it all or is just starting to amass a fortune isn't an easy task. That's why buying a collection of small items to make a custom gift basket serves two functions: It lets your creative genius shine through, and it thrills the receiver with a gift that's made especially for him or her. Look at these designs for inspiration to create your own special occasion baskets.

NEW YEAR'S DAY

Most people love January 1. It's a day to start anew and resolve to do better in life, both personally and professionally. That's what this New Year's basket reflects. After a night of revelry or a quiet evening at home watching the ball drop in Times Square, many feel that this is the time to "clean up their act." That includes any-

thing from reducing their weight to starting a business to ending nonhealthy habits. This basket focuses on setting goals while providing the receiver with a good breakfast to enjoy while pondering how to live better in the new year.

Look for light, cheerful colors to celebrate the event. A large, whitewashed basket separated into four inner sections houses this New Year's design. One section is divided lengthwise in the front, while the three remaining sections are in back. Floral foam cutting would have been too complex for this basket, so packing paper and purple-colored shred have been used for product support.

A gold-and-white table runner was doubled before insertion and draped over the basket's front in a triangular shape. Some designers roll place mats, runners, and napkins, tying them in the middle with curling ribbon and inserting them into the basket along with the other

Two glasses are tied to the basket's handle without touching.

products. A great time to buy these items printed with the words HAPPY NEW YEAR is between January and March when stores discount such products in hopes of recouping their money. Dollar stores may also sell such items early in the year.

This package represents goodies to eat for breakfast and items for healthy snacking while the recipient plans yearly goals and aspirations. In the front row are blueberry syrup, buttermilk pancake mix, peach cobbler syrup, and lemon straws. The back includes a large bottle of Bloody Mary mix, a scone mix, and white cheddar popcorn. The handle supports two glasses secured with purple curling ribbon. The glasses are tied together in such a way that neither will touch the other. If the glasses were closer, a glue dot would be placed between them to prevent breakage.

New Year's Day is one of the few times

that a diet pig wand (shown on page 88), will be appreciated and taken in the spirit in which it's given. In other words, the recipient is likely to see it as a fun gift and not one implying that the person needs to lose weight. The wand includes instructions that tells the receiver to wave it over each meal and snack to remove all calories. A HAPPY NEW YEAR pick sits on the left side within the basket's weave. Such picks serve to name the basket without additional indication from any of the products. This design is also terrific for birthday, thank-you, congratulations, and a dozen more themes. All you need is a small pick similar to the one for New Year's to state the purpose. Other embellishments include a flower pick on the right and a silver star spray in back between the two mixes. These enhancements show how to embellish without overpowering the products.

Resolutions play a big part in determining what to put into a New Year's basket, as well as the person's lifestyle, marital status, and recreational activities. Consider adding journals, healthy snacks, travel aids, store gift certificates, and magazines. Inverted top hats and fabric-covered boxes are two of the many containers that also make a great presentation.

I once showed a New Year's gift basket on The Food Network using many of these same items fastened to an oval-shaped silver serving tray. Cardboard covered with tissue paper sat within the tray to protect it from scarring. Each product was set alongside the others, which served to keep all products upright. Embellishments were added to small pieces of floral foam covered with tissue. The foam was fastened to the cardboard with glue dots. Designing with flat trays takes more time than traditional baskets, but it can make a wonderful gift that the recipient will recall the following New Year.

The Valentine's Day basket.

Products spicy, exotic, . . .

. . . romantic, and traditional can fill a Valentine's basket.

VALENTINE'S DAY

There's a group of women in Illinois who make gift baskets only during special holidays. Valentine's Day is one of these events. About a month before February 14, the women visit every discount store in the region, gathering as many low-cost items as possible. When the baskets are ready, they're sold at the busiest intersections.

Men are the biggest targets, because they usually wait until the last minute to buy a gift. And they don't buy just one; they'll select baskets for a spouse or girlfriend, mother, mother-in-law, aunt, and grandmother. Pricing their baskets at $20 to $25 each, these enterprising women make thousands of dollars in less than a week. It's a lot of work, but the payoff is worth the hours it takes to make a product that sells quickly.

Valentine's Day is one of the three most popular occasions to buy a gift basket. While some individuals stay true to the standard box of chocolates, others prefer to find items that evoke passion, show affection, or rekindle a relationship. Each year manufacturers create romantic new products to pair with old favorites, some of which are shown in this delightful Valentine's Day design.

This medium-sized oval basket is sprayed red and trimmed with a gold border. It's packed with paper and topped in red-colored shred. Love and Kisses shortbread cookies are surrounded by "Hot Hunk" beef jerky, wild-cherry-flavored body frosting, chocolate calligraphy (with paintbrush and instructions written on an attached scroll), passion mood chocolates, a Valentine's Day poem book, lover's tea bags, and a Love Map, which highlights the history of the world's great lovers. The body frosting is made to top ice cream or fruit. Like the chocolate calligraphy, it can also be painted onto a person's body.

Here's an example of star spray that's available in a shape other than stars on a wire. This embellishment contains filled and open hearts that were wrapped around a Magic Marker to create circular shapes. A rose and baby's breath pick are inserted on the right, and a bow made with punchinello ribbon is added at the back. The bow was made with a Bowdabra machine, available at many craft stores. Punchinello is a very forgiving ribbon. This same bow traveled in my suitcase to Dallas, Los Angeles, and Chicago before I added it to this design. It lay between my clothes, flat as a Frisbee, and still looks great.

Exotic goodies aren't the only products to include for that special someone. Low-cost treats continue to be Valentine's Day favorites. Red Hots, Hershey's Kisses, Fireballs, and heart-shaped candies imprinted with messages make terrific gifts. Boxes of chocolate fit snugly into many small and medium-sized baskets. Gifts, such as the Love Map and poem book, should also be sought. Heart-shaped sponges or pillows, massage or day spa certificates, a love music CD, and heart-shaped picture frames lovingly complete this basket. Also consider giving the Spa basket, shown in chapter 8 (see page 80), for Valentine's Day. An ice bucket, heart-shaped box, or anything made with brass makes a great container if a basket isn't grand enough.

My second guest appearance on The Food Network was to show Valentine's Day gifts. Most items had to be foods, of course, but I added some unique gift items among the edibles. I showed gifts made on silver serving trays, in a heart-shaped red pocketbook made from cardboard, and on an oval brass container similar to what Godiva uses for its deluxe cookie tin. One gift, made specifically for an expectant mother, was cookies, biscotti, and tea tucked into a mug made in the shape of a pregnant woman's stomach. It might sound strange, but it was a big hit with the show hosts and individuals who called to order. Leftover mugs were made into Mother's Day gifts.

Remember to look for plush animals for your Valentine's Day baskets. One of my best sellers was a "Prisoner of Love" dog. It was white with black stripes, had a dark circle around its left eye, a ball and chain on one ankle, and a white prison shirt with an inmate's number on the back. The dog was one item I could never keep enough of in stock. People bought it individually and for basket inclusion. Unfortunately, the company that made it stopped production.

A Valentine's Day basket is a very personal gift that expresses the world's most powerful emotion. Choose your products carefully, and the creation will express sentiments better than a box of chocolates.

The Mother's Day basket.

MOTHER'S DAY

There are times when a traditional basket is enough to create a Mother's Day design. Other times, however, you must have a container that's as unique as the woman who will receive it. The wooden wheelbarrow for the design shown here was chosen because moms are in charge of 99 percent of household duties. Therefore, she needs an extra pair of hands, or at least a vessel that represents a friendly helper. I remember the days when my arms were filled with my daughter, two bags of groceries, and an umbrella. A wheelbarrow would have been dandy.

This container is a candidate for either packing paper or floral foam. The choice depends on how deep the products are within the wheelbarrow and if anything is in danger of tipping out before it's wrapped. This design uses tissue-wrapped floral foam and green-colored shred. Several products require skewers. The open weave requires you to place tissue paper along the inside of the basket before adding the filling. This tissue is printed with spring flowers, enhancing the garden theme that the wheelbarrow also represents.

Floral foam was used to construct this basket. The tallest products—corn snacks and pasta—are tucked into the back.

Inside this basket are an easy-to-make pasta dinner, corn snacks, peanut brittle, cookies, crackers, two types of wine jelly, cheese spread, and an imprinted mug. Long-stemmed yellow roses are added on the right, and faux green grapes sit between the products in the front and on the left. The mug contains flowers that were made by my daughter, Genesis, for a school project. Alternate mug items are tea or other beverage of Mom's choice, cookies, or hard candies.

One jar of wine jelly is stacked atop the cookie can; two glue dots keep the jelly in place. The pasta meal and corn snacks are tucked into the space between the wheelbarrow and floral foam. There's no need for skewers, as used with the other products. Mugs are flat and easily added to most designs. Glue dots help hold the mug in place on top of the crackers. An alternative location for the mug is where the cheese spread stands, leaving the spread to be added atop the crackers.

Your product selection should encourage Mom to relax and enjoy the day. It may not be possible, especially with today's hectic pace, but the thought will be appreciated. This is an occasion where items that Mom truly loves should be the only products included. Look for stationery, writing instruments, and journals if she writes personal notes or jots down ideas. An organizer that keeps these items in one place is a potential container. Is she a collector of lace or figurines? Consider adding that type of gift. Perhaps baking is her passion. Cookie cutters, a cake plate (potential container), a matching apron and mitt, a recipe book, and parchment paper should be high on your list. If she's ready for a handheld organizer, they're available for low prices and are small enough to fit in her purse. What about the professional mom? Personalized luggage tags, a monogrammed business card holder, a travel alarm clock, a wallet to hold her passport, and other valuables will be appreciated.

A hat box is another container she'll treasure. It should be a keepsake item, such as the one made with brocade fabric and velveteen used to create the Chocoholics basket in chapter 10 (see page 122). This is another container that was a customer favorite. One person ordered six Mother's Day baskets using the hat box. Each was filled with candles, perfumes, soaps, drawer and closet sachets, room fresheners, bubble bath, lotions, and heart-shaped mirrors, all with a specific fragrance for each recipient. Flowers that corresponded with the scents lined the box. The gifts were shipped as far as the Canary Islands, so the arrangements were shrink-wrapped and covered with printed cellophane to make a dazzling presentation.

Another person wanted a gift basket for a mom who loves lottery scratch-off tickets. He gave me a hundred tickets and asked that I make what he called a "basket of luck." I wrapped each ticket in cellophane and attached them all to individual skewers. The tickets looked like lollipops, which I inserted into floral foam. The cellophane was closed with an enormous bow and a card that read, "I'm lucky to have you as a mom."

This special lady screamed with joy when I delivered the basket on Mother's Day. She invited me into her home and immediately called her son. Her voice stayed at a high pitch—so much so that a neighbor alerted the police. They arrived soon after, but the woman never calmed down. She invited the police inside to see her basket of luck. I was ready to leave to spend the day with my own mom, but as luck would have it, one of the policemen asked if I could make the same gift for his own mother, with the addition of coffee and scones. It takes a while to wrap individual lottery tickets, so his gift was delivered the next day. Mother's Day gift baskets are a joy to create, and it's wonderful to get a glimpse of the love between a mother and her children.

Make Mom's favorite things the focal point of your search, and don't stop until you find the items she adores. Her reaction will be worth it.

The Father's Day basket.

This Father's Day basket focuses on that men's favorite: open-and-eat snacks. Few embellishments are needed, though cattails and a wildflower pick add interest.

FATHER'S DAY

Making a Father's Day gift seems easier than creating one for Mother's Day. That's because most retail stores treat all dads the same way. They've convinced customers that dads should receive ties, money clips, cologne, a pack of briefs, socks, and that square piece of wood on which keys and spare change are placed. Most dads won't balk at receiving these items, but with gift baskets, you can do much better.

Some dads are happy on this special day to tinker around their favorite toys—cars, wide-screen televisions, a pool table, or a variety of electronic gadgets. Others get together with friends they haven't seen in months. Then there are the dads who are content to stand guard over a grill after almost destroying the kitchen during preparation.

Most men, though, are fans of open-and-eat foods, and that's the focus of this Father's Day basket. A rectangular country basket with green trim provides the foundation and makes an attractive appearance no matter where Dad lives, be it in a rural or city setting. The laid-back lifestyle of most dads means that floral foam and skewers aren't needed here. Although the basket contains several openings within the weave, tissue paper wasn't a necessity. The brown packing paper topped with purple-colored shred corresponded well with this design.

There's no quiche in this Dad's basket, but some men enjoy this cheesy meal, so add it if it's one of his favorite foods. This design contains a beef steak stick, caramel popcorn, seasoned nuts, combination beef jerky and cheese sticks, dipping pretzels, mustard, and a beer bread mix in a tall glass bottle. The mix is simple to make and can be served during Father's Day dinner. I never met a man who didn't want to tear away the cellophane and dive into flavorful snacks. If this sounds like your husband, dad, or other significant male, this basket is for him.

A favorite beverage, disposable camera to capture the day's festivities, a mug, sports video, a pouch to hold the remote control and television guide, grooming tools, a car wash kit, and a picture frame to place a family photo are other options for Dad's basket. As with a basket for Mom, adding his preferences is important to make the day special. Perhaps he favors a certain fragrance that's available as a soap, cologne, after-shower spray, and powder. That makes a marvelous basket, but as with other designs, don't combine these items in the same basket with food. Either give Dad two small baskets separated by items to eat and items to wear, or select just one group of many items that can be paired together.

Basket substitutes run the gamut. A toolbox, snack bowl, car organizer, decorative wastebasket for his favorite area, and bucket for car washing provide ample room for gift placement. I've created Father's Day baskets for busy executives

using open briefcases filled with writing instruments, notepads, an antistress toy, several business magazines, a business card holder, and bags of healthy snacks.

You'll notice that this basket isn't filled with many enhancements. Most men aren't fans of frills. They're excited about the snacks and gifts, not flora and fauna. This design is limited to two cattails and a small wildflower pick that matches the shred's color. Don't add much more than this to your Father's Day basket unless the recipient appreciates embellishments.

Designers don't receive as many calls for Dad's Day baskets as they do for Mother's Day, but they stay prepared for the few orders received. Their inventory includes a variety of sweet, savory, and peppery products that are normally added to all-occasion baskets. Fishing box and tool caddy baskets are purchased by real estate salesmen and relocation specialists who thank their clients using containers that match recipients' lifestyles. They learn a lot about customers through the initial prequalification meeting and subsequent gatherings. When designers find a bargain on baskets and containers that create good-looking men's designs, they buy a collection knowing that both individuals and corporate buyers will order.

Men are seldom choosy when it comes to basket contents. As long as you include a collection of great-tasting foods, he'll award you with "two thumbs up," meaning the basket is a winner.

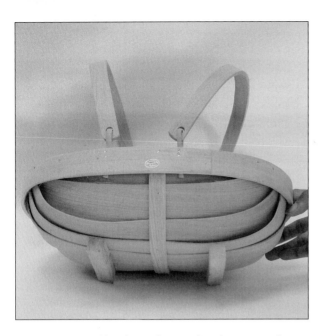

Shaped to resemble a boat, this vessel makes a great foundation for a Fourth of July gift basket.

A mix of "eat now, make later" products will come in handy at a July 4 picnic.

JULY 4

It starts with a hot summer day made hotter by the mandatory grill-cooked hamburgers and a kettle of baked beans. But then you reach into the basket of summer snacks that arrived yesterday. It's complete with assorted lemonade mixes, homemade peanut brittle, lemon-slice candies, buttery popcorn, and an assortment of penny candies that remind you of your childhood. The children race through the backyard, playing with the pinwheels and blowing bubbles that were also stashed in the basket. As you grab a slice of watermelon and press a cold glass of lemonade to your forehead, you think about the evening's festivities, sitting in a lounge chair and watching the fireworks from your second-floor balcony with that basket of snacks at your fingertips.

Independence Day stands out as a significant holiday for Americans. Wars abroad and tragic circumstances in New York and Washington, DC, have in recent years helped place more focus on family ties and taking nothing in our lives for granted. American memorabilia in country and contemporary styles is a big business, which makes creating a July 4 gift basket as simple as blowing on a pinwheel. Red, white, and blue are colors you'll find in lots of product packaging. That's another fact that makes finding appropriate products easy.

The basket depicted here is crafted to resemble a boat. It's curved on both sides and contains feet on the bottom as if the basket is in permanent dry dock. The handles fall to the sides and help augment the container. Because of the curved bottom, it's easier to place red-colored shred on top of packing paper rather than making a mess by cutting floral foam into shape.

A mix of "eat now, make later" products can be used to fill this basket. A shrimp dip, peanut brittle, corn snacks, cookies, clam dip kit, snack mix, grill seasonings, assorted beverages, and a flavored teaspoon proudly represent the day. Rather than use glue dots to keep each product upright, an extra layer of shred holds each product in place. Try setting a plastic election campaign hat atop the products, fastened with glue dots. It's an item that you may have in your basement or attic waiting for a great basket design to adorn. Add two star sprays made with white onion grass and red and blue stars. Small flags are another enhancement that will fit the occasion.

Patriotic items are perfect, but there's much more to consider for this design. Look for a horn or bugle, a CD of patriotic music, a Statue of Liberty figurine, small packages of apple pie, American-themed bumper stickers, historic books, freezer pops for the children, and thong slippers. An upturned top hat makes a good container, as would a ceramic watermelon bowl or apple pie plate.

My designing friends in the Southern California area are pros at making July 4 baskets using tabletop barbecue grills as the container. The grills, which are sold for less than $5.00 each, are purchased from local drugstores that sell each with utensils and squirt bottles for ketchup, mustard, and relish. Once one drugstore's stock is depleted, they move on to others within the chain, grabbing grills until the summer ends or the inventory is gone, whichever comes first. Not only do customers order these custom creations for relatives whom they cannot visit during the holiday, but the designers also receive many orders from workers in the home construction and decorating industries.

A July 4 basket can be combined with summer items such as plates, bowls, cups, and napkins. These products are usually placed at the back of the basket, while the snacks sit in front. Barbecue sauces, corncob holders, an ice cream scooper, cones, and toppings are summertime fixings that shouldn't be overlooked. Super Soakers, bat and balls, and jump ropes are fun toys to add for children, as long as each is safe for the targeted age group.

Independence Day has a different meaning for every person, and gift baskets are versatile enough to incorporate something for everyone. Try creating one that's patriotic and another that encompasses the meaning of summer. You'll make someone's turn at the grill a lot easier.

The Christmas basket.

The handle tilted in back of this country basket helps to secure the contents.

The snowman on this mug's handle spins when it's touched.

CHRISTMAS

A Christmas basket has the power to make an adult race alongside the children to see what's under the tree. I know one woman who, after receiving a gift basket in 1994, doesn't feel the holiday is complete without getting at least one basket of gifts. It might be placed under the tree, or a relative could be charged with bringing it to the dinner festivities. She'll even allow the use of the same basket, as long as it's filled with a few trinkets and decorated with cellophane, ribbons, balloons, and bows. It's a tradition she hopes will be continued forever.

Christmas is, by far, the number one holiday for gift basket giving. Individuals and corporations order them by the dozens. Friends, family, coworkers, and employees look forward to peeling back the cellophane closure to find a variety of gifts and treats in appreciation of support, friendship, or a job well done during the year. Personal and corporate gift baskets often include the same items—except, of course, when it comes to personal care products and intimate apparel. While it's appropriate for friends to exchange perfumes and fragrances, corporations steer clear of buying these very personal items. They may, however, offer a gift certificate to a department store where the recipient can choose personal goods without the company's knowledge.

This holiday basket is fun and easy to make. It can be created in a taller basket,

or you can add dozens of extra items for one person or an entire family. Floral foam is added underneath the red-colored shred, but you can keep the design simple by using packing paper. Foam was chosen because the accompanying skewers help support the mug and also keep the pasta package at an angle.

The wooden country basket is trimmed in green. Its handle is positioned in the back and raised slightly to secure the products. Chili pepper pasta, Christmas tea, mixed nuts, holiday cookies, and a large snowman mug create a well-rounded gift for a man or woman. A holiday pick is placed in the middle directly in front of the cookies, and red ting-ting is added at the back. If you didn't use floral foam in this design, place a small piece in back to anchor the enhancement. Packing paper would not be enough to secure the ting-ting.

A holiday swag made with gold-sprayed and green leaves, pinecones, and curls is shaped to sit around the basket's front. Each of the swag's ends is bent around the basket's handles and tucked on the inside. A similar method is used for the grapevine attached to the Get-Well basket in chapter 7 (see page 73). The entire swag is wired, so it can be twisted and arranged as needed. Swags are found in craft stores, usually in the same area with picks and other decorative enhancements.

Mugs have evolved from one-color containers to embellished gifts. Some mugs magically change colors when hot beverages are poured in. This "Spinner

Christmas-themed cookies are a popular addition to gift baskets and can be left out for Santa on Christmas Eve.

Mug" was named for the addition of a decorative item on the handle: The snowman spins when touched. I've used a similar mug with a casino theme for a retirement gift. The spinner piece was a single die on the handle, and the retiree said that it was too pretty to use. Your receiver may say the same about the snowman mug, but that's okay. Some baskets and their contents may never be opened, let alone used.

It's wonderful to see pasta in unique shapes, and even if you buy the traditionally straight noodles, many are in colors that denote the flavor. The pasta here is shaped to resemble chili peppers. It might be added to a southwestern Christmas basket, or perhaps the receiver loves trying something new and will make it sometime in the New Year. What do you think about the cookies with the stocking stamped on the face? Children are sure to get a "kick" out of leaving these and milk on a table in the hope that Santa will leave gifts under the tree.

Basket alternatives include a stocking, punch bowl, gift box, coffee- or teapot, and large mug. An ice bucket was my clients' favorite container. It was aluminized and sprayed in gold, green, or silver. Champagne, glasses, a heart-shaped pillow, and a month's supply of bubble bath were given by a husband to his spouse.

It's difficult to share ideas for Christmas baskets. As with a birthday basket and other arrangements, the chosen products will depend on the receiver's preferences. They may also depend on whether the person was naughty or nice.

The Hanukkah basket.

HANUKKAH

I was unfamiliar with making Hanukkah baskets until several clients requested gifts for customers who celebrate the tradition. Hanukkah, a religious event (the word is Hebrew for "dedication"), is an event celebrated for eight days and nights. It commemorates the victory over the Syrian armies in 165 B.C.E. One candle on the menorah is lit on each of the eight days. The Shamash, the highest candle, is used to light the others, and blessings are restated each night before the lighting.

Many of the companies from which I purchased products also sold kosher items (as evident by the KOSHER symbol on the package's back), and that made the selection easier as I filled my clients' orders. The basket size wasn't huge, nor was it required to be. Each had to show appreciation for the year's business. The baskets were mailed either to a small office or to the client's home and included enough items to share with a spouse or office staff.

As with creating a Kwanzaa basket (see page 108), I did some research to ensure that the color selection was appropriate. Blue and silver dominate the color scheme, so I chose products and supplies of those hues. The client was pleased with his customers' responses, and I was able to broaden my specialty designs to reflect a new group of baskets.

Kosher products of all kinds are a natural choice for Hanukkah baskets.

A silver serving tray positioned in back complements the color scheme and makes a lovely keepsake.

An open weave basket is used for this Hanukkah design. The weave is particularly wide, and the blue tissue paper is visible between the openings. White tissue is also included. I added packing paper before topping the basket with gold and white shred. Blue shred was another option, but the gold and white mix makes a dynamic contrast against the tissue paper. This medium-sized basket pairs well with the items, which are tightly packed to create a stable and upright design.

The kosher products in this basket are fudge-filled walnut cookies, a small cake, orange thimble cookies, a ready-to-make pasta meal, vanilla pecan tea cookies, and an oval-shaped silver tray. The tray creates a decorative addition and can be used to serve the cakes and cookies within the basket. One silver star spray is placed on the right. A shorter, silver pick is an option in front, and silver tissue paper is a substitute for the blue-and-white tissue combination.

Menorah candles, dreidels, and children's books that explain the history of Hanukkah are other items that fit into this design. Latkes, gelt (chocolate coins), cheese blintzes, *sufganiyot* (jelly doughnuts without the hole), and other food items with the kosher stamp of approval can be incorporated within this mix to create an impressive arrangement. Such a basket must be hand-delivered rather than shipped, because most of these foods require immediate refrigeration. The only time it can be shipped is when the dry ingredients to make traditional Hanukkah foods are mailed.

Couples who are celebrating their first Hanukkah together may appreciate a basket that includes a menorah and candles. Such baskets need to be long rather than wide and aren't more expensive than traditional baskets. Containers are another option. You may find corrugated boxes with Star of David symbols depicted on the front and back. Large, two-piece dreidels are capable of holding a collection of celebratory products. There are also companies that specialize in Hanukkah goods with a wide variety of items for adults and children—items that are perfect for gift basket inclusion.

If a basket isn't appropriate, tote bags are another handy item to create a Hanukkah present. A tote lined with a coordinating tissue and filled with a packing paper foundation is the beginning of a thoughtful gift. My former insurance agent ordered such a bag with four kosher items including nuts and biscotti. She distributed the totes to more than a hundred clients, who were pleased that she showed appreciation for selecting her as their agent. Not all of these clients celebrated Hanukkah, but the products were universal to most taste buds. These gifts were very easy to create and took less time than designing a hundred baskets, although of course the latter would have been just as beautiful.

The Kwanzaa basket.

KWANZAA

Kwanzaa is a nonreligious event that occurs from December 26 to January 1. It was created in 1966 by Dr. Maulana Karenga to celebrate African-American heritage. Kwanzaa is not an alternative to Christmas, and because it's not based on religion, people from all backgrounds are welcome to celebrate this occasion. The seven principles of Kwanzaa, known as the Nguzo Saba (a Swahili term that means "first fruits"), are recited each day, and the participants use the principles to reflect on their family, community, and heritage.

A Kwanzaa basket is based on items with an African or Caribbean background. You'll find an abundance of products that contain African-based colors and symbols available, some of which are shown in this Kwanzaa basket. The vessel is African in origin and serves to theme this wonderful design. It's made from three pieces of cloth sewn together with thin leather cord on the sides and bottom. A tricolored

A glue dot is used to anchor the products.

Museum shops make a good source for Kwanzaa-themed products.

braided rope is secured around the basket's rim. Two strands of beads dangle in front, or the beads can be positioned on the side or back.

The contents include a rum cake, a pyramid-shaped paperweight, a book containing African proverbs, a business card holder and notebook with hieroglyphics stamped on the front and back covers, four coasters made from African material, a cosmetic purse set made with African material, and a small black pocketbook with a patch of the African continent sewn in the middle.

The products are elevated with packing paper on the basket's inside, topped with beige-colored shred, which is pushed down slightly so that the braid around the basket remains visible. Black, gold, brown, beige, green, and red are the colors that tie this theme together. Glue dots are used to anchor the products together. Notice the glue dot placement between the business card holder and rum cake package. There aren't many embellishments within this design, but few are needed. A few pieces of ting-ting and wild grass are added in back for height.

Alternate containers include boxes in colors of black, red, green or gold. General baskets are also useful; the products will create the Kwanzaa theme. Figurines, pyramid-shaped candies or chocolates, home decor items (table runners, napkins, cloths, and the like), adult and children's books, CDs of African music, and African

coffee are Kwanzaa basket items found in stores. Museums and specialty shops are good places to find items that are African-based. The notebook and business card holder were made especially for the Brooklyn (New York) Museum, a place where many Egyptian antiquities are on permanent display.

It used to be difficult to find Kwanzaa products that were affordable while reflecting tradition. Now that many cultural traditions are embraced within the United States and abroad, it's become easier to find items that denote the African experience. Wholesalers make food and gift items for various cultures, which can be found in local stores around the country.

Several designers specialize in Kwanzaa baskets, especially in areas where there's a large concentration of African-American residents. Their clients look forward to the celebration and present gifts when traveling or to each person within a family. One designer located in the Midwest creates Kwanzaa baskets using a plain white box and mudcloth or kente fabric. She covers the box and then glues the fabric into place. It's an inexpensive method that creates a stunning design, which sells briskly at year's end.

You may not have a need to make Kwanzaa baskets, but you will become more aware of the products that create this celebratory theme when you are looking for items for all-occasion baskets.

Rocking chairs make ideal vessels for retirement gifts.

Chapter 10

THINK OUT OF
THE BASKET

Alternative Containers Challenge Your Creativity

Baskets will always be the main vessel for our gifts, but other types of containers have become just as popular in recent years. People love receiving a container they can reuse in a foyer, bedroom, dining area or other location in or out of the home. Flowerpots, vases, wagons, tea cups, mugs, and boxes are examples of nonbasket containers that can be used to design packages.

My business was built around containers. I used rocking chairs for retirement gifts, wagons for new babies, upturned umbrellas for bridal showers, and flowerpots for gardeners. Each gift sold quickly because the buyer loved the fact that recipients would enjoy seeing the container in their homes or offices. Of course, baskets can be used more than once, too, but a container seems to add its own brand of excitement.

In September 1994 I wanted to appear on The Food Network, so I sent a producer a tea cup and saucer lined with fruit-filled cookies freshly baked by my sister, Cassandra. Each cookie was wrapped and skewered to resemble a lollipop. The entire design was closed in cellophane, and I drove to the show's studio on Sixth Avenue in New York to present it along with printed materials about my company.

The producer called an hour after I delivered the design. He was interested in having me as a guest on a show but wasn't able to find time. Another producer saw my information, and I appeared on another show on December 26, 1994. The audience was treated to New Year's gifts designed in top hats, briefcases, silver-plated trays, and wine buckets. That three-minute appearance exposed my containered gifts to more than twenty-two million viewers worldwide. I received calls from people who not only wanted more information but also from those who ordered on the spot. It was an extraordinary experience that proved how much people adore containers.

The Fruit-Decorated box.

The key lime–flavored treats and fruit-covered cup and saucer continue the fruit theme.

FRUIT-DECORATED BOX

Boxes create magnificent gifts. They're available in many shapes and used for various purposes. Some are specifically for hats, and others hold jewelry, clothing, or shoes. Interior designers choose nested boxes to embellish living space corners. You'll see these boxes stacked atop each other in sets of three, four, or five, all in the same pattern. They're usually square in shape, but some are oval.

A box is rigid enough to hold anything. It will support an item as light as a pen or as heavy as a bottle of cider. The square box you see here, decorated in apples, pears, cherries, lemons, and grapes, is great for celebrating birthdays, wishing good luck, saying thank-you, offering as a housewarming, and more. It's covered in paper rather than fabric. The finish contains a slightly raised pattern. The vertical perforations are also visible if you look closely at the box and lid.

Inside this box are Bavarian-style pretzels, key lime mustard, key-lime-flavored cookies, and a cup and saucer. A beverage isn't always required because a cup is included. Perhaps the person who will receive this gift has broken a favorite saucer set, and this one is a replacement. Others may prefer a specific blend of coffee or tea to which you have no access. If a design has no room for a beverage, but you'd still like to include one, do so in the cup.

Key lime–flavored products may remind the recipient of a vacation to a southern state or perhaps bring back childhood memories. If key lime isn't the preferred flavor, these products can be swapped for another such as tangerine, apricot, lemon, or strawberry. A pancake mix and syrup, scones, a plush toy, or stationery are suggested alternatives.

What makes this arrangement better for a woman than a man is the tea cup with saucer. Some men wouldn't mind receiving such a decorative product, but others would prefer a set in solid green or burgundy. Aside from that, it's a wonderful gift anyone would love to receive.

The box's lid creates a faux back wall. It could have been placed on the bottom to hold the box, but using the lid as a decorative "wall" is the better option. To create this look, insert the lid so that one corner peaks upward at the midpoint. The pattern should face forward. Packing paper and shred are the cushion, and both are added before or after the lid enters the box. There's no need to fill the open lid facing the back with shred or an embellishment.

When all the products are in place, a small apple and berry pick are inserted. The pretzel's bag is folded down by approximately ¼ inch at the top and taped in place. Glue dots are another way to shorten a package's height.

Boxes are extremely easy to close within cellophane, a basket bag, or shrink

The box's lid creates a faux back wall. Set the lid facing forward.

wrap. Use the cellophane closing technique described in chapter 6 as a guide (see page 44). The bottom corners create ninety-degree angles that keep the closure material smooth and tight on all sides. There's no need to fold gaps to be taped underneath—the corner edges ensure a clean presentation.

You can find similar boxes at card stores, boutique shops, and chain stores such as Target and Wal-Mart. Don't be surprised if office suppliers offer boxes on their clearance table after the holidays. Chocolates, cookies, candies, and a variety of containers are the first items to go on sale after December 25. Review the prices, and decide if such goods are worth buying.

When the recipient removes all of the products, the decorated box becomes a handy reusable container. A man can use the box to organize his favorite colognes or bathroom toiletries. A woman might arrange teas and accessories (tea strainer, spoons, cubed sugar, honey sticks, what have you) under the lid. Potpourri, nail care items, and plush animals are other items that might be stored in the empty box.

The Thank-You box.

THANK-YOU BOX

Here's a box with lots of character. The design has universal appeal by expressing thanks in several languages. This is one of the first boxes I used to create a gift ordered by a principal for his staff. All had experienced a disconcerting school year due to huge changes in personnel, including the principal's job. He asked me to make one gift for each of his twenty-five teachers and six office staff members. Everyone received the Thank-You box, customized according to each person's age

and lifestyle. Making thirty-one different designs wasn't as difficult as it sounds. Some individuals received the same type of popcorn or cookies, but one staffer played golf, and another loved word puzzles. The differences made each container shine, and so did the recipients when they received the gifts.

The box's solid construction holds products sturdily and won't collapse during transit. Unlike similarly made smaller boxes with a straight brim, as shown throughout this chapter, this container's upper edge is notched in the front and back. You should

This box is sturdy enough to hold hefty products with ease.

Decorative fans placed in back are the only embellishment this design needs.

always fill this box with paper; you'd simply need too many foam bricks to elevate the products. Beige or vanilla-colored shred is too bland for this pretty container. Red was chosen, but blue, green, or yellow would be just as vivid.

It's easy to read the contents' labels except for one—the scone mix. Caramel popcorn, spice cookies, the baking mix, a wine jelly assortment, roasted red pepper jam, and New York–style cheesecake fill the box. A Realtor would adore this type of design to present to a new homeowner. A friend who's been supportive through a crisis is another deserving recipient. It's also a great way for newlyweds to express their appreciation to both sets of parents. This gift or a smaller version containing three or four items may be the right size for a neighbor who retrieves the mail and newspaper while you're on vacation. There's someone in your life who deserves this gift.

Decorative fans are the only enhancement added to the design. They serve as a striking backdrop while supporting the three products in back. Other embellishments are acceptable, but there are times when less is better. The ribbon tied around the box of assorted wine jellies is a pretty and decorative touch. Many manufacturers embellish their products in this manner, and so can you. It's a way to add class to the entire design by using just one piece of ribbon.

This design is beautiful because of its simplicity. There are no stacking or positioning dilemmas; three products are placed next to each other in two rows. Finding products that theme well together and fit within a container's width isn't an easy task. As you become accustomed to gift basket making, however, you'll develop a sense for selecting products that create beautiful arrangements in a fair amount of time. A gift basket that takes you forty-five minutes the first time will take thirty minutes the next and fifteen minutes thereafter.

As with the fruit box, you'll find any of the popular cellophane closures to be a satisfactory choice. Basket bags are made solely to fit this box. If you'll be shipping the gift out of town, you might consider using a two-pronged wrapping solution of shrink wrap first, then a soft cellophane covering.

Thank-you gifts should also include treats for four-legged friends if they are part of the household. One designer bought a set of bones in Styrofoam packaging that resembled supermarket-style meat. It was closed in plastic wrap and tied with a pretty bow. She added it to her customer's basket after finding out that the recipient owned a dog. The receiver was thrilled because the prized pooch was acknowledged.

The Thanksgiving box.

This box stores flat when not in use . . .

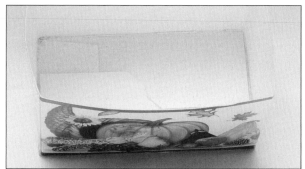

. . . then sets up easily, ready to be filled.

THANKSGIVING BOX

Giving thanks is not only practiced at home but also shared when invited to another person's house. Or perhaps you're someone who distributes Thanksgiving gifts rather than baskets for Christmas. Small, printed boxes make a friendly substitute for a basket. They allow men and women to present or receive gifts that don't leave the impression of going to Grandma's house.

The container shown here is a breeze to style. Designers love this sturdy paper box because it stores flat when not in use and sets up easily by twisting the bottom connectors into place. The large box shown in the Thank-You design is just as simple to store (see page 115). The Thanksgiving box holds four to five products, depending on size, and wraps easily within cellophane or a custom-sized basket

Packing paper is used to fill the box, although floral foam would work just as well.

bag. One floral foam brick fits perfectly in the bottom if skewers are preferred to anchor each product. Packing paper secures each item just as well, and that's the method used here. Orange-colored shred matches the colors on the box. If the person who's to receive this doesn't celebrate Thanksgiving, there's also a box designed with fall leaves, an appropriate choice for individuals from other cultures.

What Thanksgiving hostess wouldn't appreciate receiving a selection of items that she can sit back and enjoy during the weekend? Seasoned pretzels, spicy dip, apple pie jam, and tangerine-orange cookies make a tasty treat when the recipient is tired of turkey. The apple pie jam pairs well with pancakes and crackers and can be used as a pretzel dip, depending on the recipient's taste buds. A magnetic or cubed notepad, small wall plaque, meat rub and seasonings, unscented candles, and mixed nuts are other options for this package.

This gift contains no enhancements, but it's not noticeable. It's another design with a full load of products that would, in effect, be interrupted by picks and stems. The box shows a festive harvest scene, and the contents' packaging matches the box and shred colors. Bright, cheery gifts need few or no enhancements.

A Thanksgiving package should be created as a gesture of gratitude toward a friend or loved one. Keep the gift simple by choosing items that are quick to open and easy to use.

The striking Black-and-White-Striped box is always in fashion.

*Printed cellophane and
a mesh bow add
the finishing touches.*

BLACK-AND-WHITE-STRIPED BOX

When I see black and white, I think of fashion. No matter what colors are in vogue, basic black and white will always be on the runway. Such classic colors are the focus for this boxed gift. The Thanksgiving box featured a holiday design full of light colors, but boxes can present a timeless appearance. The black-and-white stripes might also be viewed as a corporate look—something you'd give to, say, an executive. A second marriage, college graduation, or other types of personal achievement are also appropriate occasions for this style.

Shred in shades of purple, burgundy, or pink presents a striking contrast to this box design, as well as products with packaging that highlights similar colors. This gift and its contents focus on the black-and-white format. Packing paper fills the bottom, topped with mixed white and gold shred. Peanut brittle, orange walnut cookies, double fudge cookies, chocolate dipping sauce, and a plastic cone filled with ice cream toppings create a delicious assortment that's great for any occasion.

Friends often ask me for men's gifts ideas, and I suggest this type of design. Cattails can replace the flowered pick on the left, or enhancements can be omitted entirely. It's a simple, couch-potato-type box of treats to enjoy while watching a favorite television show or rented movie.

The jar of dipping fudge is weighty and initially sank down into the box so that its label was covered. Extra packing paper was added to the space, and shred was placed on top before repositioning the fudge. It now sits tall without wobbling so that the recipient will see the label. This was easy to do, especially because raising the jar didn't affect the fudge cookies' box. The same technique was shown in chapter 4 to elevate jam (see page 32). Cellophane is used to close this basket, and the gold mesh bow adds elegance.

A small basket is just as simple to use for this design, but it's great to see alternatives to using traditional vessels. All of us want to show our creativity when giving gifts, whether that means finding a product with exotic flavoring or a container that's new and unique. It's what makes my creations so appealing. Eventually, you'll find people saying the same about yours.

Always look for beautiful baskets and unique containers that keep your design style fresh and inspiring. Consider anything with an open middle as the start of your masterpiece.

The Chocoholic design.

A white brocade hat box sets off this assortment of chocolate goodies.

CHOCOHOLIC DESIGN

Are you a person who craves at least one piece of chocolate every day? Join the club. Chemists tell us that this sweet treat alters a person's mood for the better, but instead of being scientific, why not make a chocoholic basket and let the recipient be the judge?

Here's the ultimate chocoholic's delight, a selection of items that are either made from chocolate, include chocolate, or are ready for dipping into chocolate. You're no doubt familiar with some of the items, but others will be a pleasant surprise. Chocolate pasta, raspberry dessert topping, seasoned pretzels, dipping fudge, tranquility chocolate confections, a one-minute microwavable chocolate cake, chocolate squares from Brussels, crème de mint chocolate cocoa, and chocolate raspberry coffee bring you as close to chocolate heaven as you can imagine.

A striking hat box in a half-moon shape and made with white brocade material creates a beautiful appearance for the products. It's accented with a white rope cord inserted into the box through two grommets. The box and lid are lined in black velvet. One floral foam brick is used in back, and packing paper lines the box's front curve and upper portion. Pink-colored shred cushions the products. Two picks in pink shades complement the shred. Glue dots stabilize the dipping fudge atop the raspberry sauce.

The box's lid is inserted into the back at an angle. It's the only way that the lid will fit properly to give the design height; placing the lid under the box would be an uncreative decision. One edge is pushed down into the box, while the other sits on top. You can see the lid's black velvet interior from the back view.

The chocolate pasta and raspberry topping are paired for eating together, although it's not mandatory. This pasta, made in spiral curl shapes, is a dessert rather than dinner. It's cooked in the traditional way, then cooled and drizzled with the sauce. Consider this an exotic treat for someone who's tasted just about everything or a sensual product that completes a Valentine's Day basket. Chocolate lovers who enjoy the combined taste of sweet and salty will dip the pretzels into the fudge sauce.

Your favorite chocoholic will love the microwavable cake, packaged with frosting, sprinkles, a candle, and a balloon. It's mixed with water in the clear, round container in which it's packaged. After microwaving it for one minute, spread the frosting, add sprinkles, light the candle (after placing it in the cake), and blow up the balloon for a personal chocoholics party. These cakes are available in many themes such as cheer up, happy birthday, and teacher, and are extremely popular in gift baskets.

Chocolate bars, chocolate snack cakes, truffles, four-piece candy boxes, chocolate

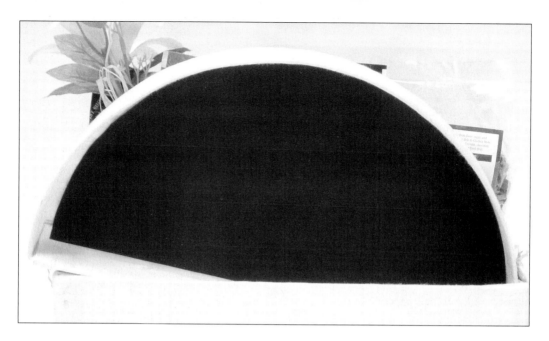

Insert the box's black-velvet-lined lid into the back with one end peeking out.

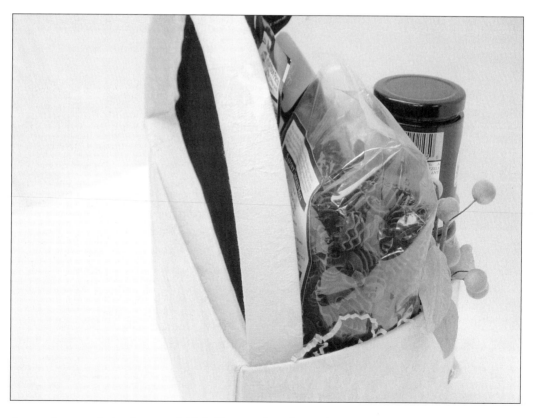

A rear view reveals the elegance of this half-moon shaped container.

Chocolate products run the gamut from classic to, well, surprising. Yes, that's chocolate pasta on the left.

bath products (chocolate items for the skin), Oreos, chocolate biscotti, and chocolate cookies should be considered for your custom design. A mix of chocolate snacks from the supermarket and chocolate goodies from upscale stores creates a balanced collection of treats to devour.

One West Coast company makes square and heart-shaped chocolate boxes—that is, the actual box is made of chocolate. Each shape is filled with round chocolate confections and coffee beans and sealed on top with a chocolate lid that sits within a molded lip. After eating the contents, the box is broken apart and eaten bit by bit. I gave my bank's manager the square-shaped box for her marriage anniversary. She called to thank me and ordered twelve boxes for clients who had recently made substantial deposits. How's that for chocolate overload?

If you live with chocoholics, be sure to tuck this design out of sight until time for delivery. That's the only way to keep you from returning to the store to buy items that mysteriously disappear.

The Tote bag.

Use packing paper to fill the bag and create a rigid foundation.

Add just a bit of shred in the bag.

Chapter 11

MORE OUT-OF-THE-BASKET DESIGNS
Totes, Trunks, Towers, and More

Baskets and boxes are just the beginning. There are many other items—some right in your own basement, attic, or garage—that can serve as beautiful containers. Here's a look at a few additional no-basket containers that can be used to create your next "gift basket" masterpiece.

TOTE BAG

Bags make a fashion statement. Many are still available in solid colors, but others are splashed with multiple hues, trimmed with lace, or adorned with beads. People love bags, so manufacturers create new styles to keep these items selling briskly in card, party, and other small shops.

Bags aren't as fragile as they appear. At first glance this paper-based item might seem unable to support a collection of products. However, the pictured bag in a burgundy Fleur de Lis pattern is a willing container for four average-weight products. Packing paper fills the bottom portion to create a rigid foundation, yet not so tightly as to distort the bag's shape. Very little shred is added before product insertion. You can place enough shred on the inside to cascade above the edge, but for this example, that would conceal the products' names.

This design serves to show gratitude. It can be presented at the door of a person who's invited you to a party, in appreciation for kindness when none was expected, or for watching a residence while the owner was away. The secondary reason for this gift is instant gratification. Cheese straws, caramelized popcorn, and thimble cookies are ready to be opened and eaten immediately. Round coasters printed with trivia questions and answers are the fourth item. For this gift, recipients must provide their own beverage and cups, but after reviewing the contents, I doubt that they'll mind.

An assortment of interesting products makes the Tote bag a lovely gesture of thanks.

Patterned cello and a burgundy bow complete this look.

Years ago designers cut cardboard to fit along the bag's four sides. Paper was added, followed by products. This gift is so simple to make that designers no longer waste time cutting cardboard. The tote won't fall so long as the products are of equal weight distributed on all sides.

The silver strand enhancement tied to the handles is called eyelash ribbon. It's wired and easy to curl, making a more elegant appearance than regular curling ribbon. If your local craft store doesn't sell eyelash ribbon, don't let that stop you from adding curling ribbon. Star spray is shown at the back.

Closing a bag is similar to closing a square container. The edges are at 90-degree angles, which makes closure simple. After folding the bag or cellophane closed, top with a bow. Add star spray above the cellophane fan for a little extra pizzazz.

I've used tote bags to combine popcorn, bowls, and napkins for post office clerks at the locations I visit most. During the country's anthrax scare in 2001, I knew that the postal workers felt vulnerable. The extra bags of popcorn in my inventory were leftovers from a gift basket design class concluded a month earlier. First, I lined the totes with tissue paper. Then I placed napkins in the bag, followed by Styrofoam dessert bowls. This allowed the two bags of popcorn, one caramel and one butter, to sit tall, and everyone could see the contents. Because the workers knew me, they were grateful to enjoy a snack from someone they trusted. Spreading a little joy was rewarding, and it helped some of our most dedicated workers get on with their lives.

Tote bags are available in many sizes and shapes. Some resemble mugs, cups and saucers, and briefcases. Others are triangular in shape, are studded with grommets, or contain rope handles rather than twisted paper. Bags are decorated with animals, insects, fruits, or flowers. Their versatility allows us to create beautiful gifts or store the bags flat until a use presents itself. And the affordable price will inspire you to create terrific tote bags.

This trunk makes an impressive presentation for high-powered clients.

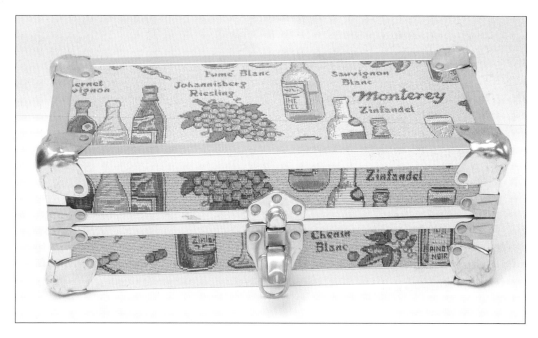

This tabletop trunk is sturdy, beautiful, and reusable.

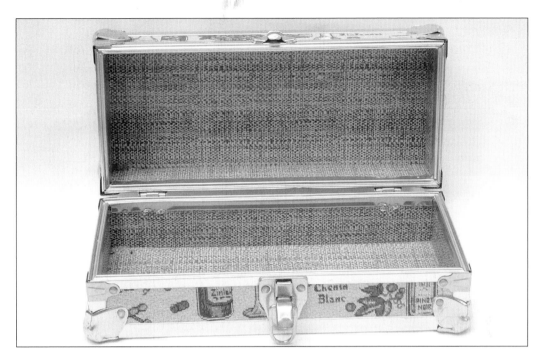

Both floral foam and packing paper make appropriate trunk fillers.

TRUNK

Beautiful containers such as this trunk are the type of object that many long to receive. You'll see shoppers pick them up and caress them in those large linen stores selling everything from candles to bedding. Then they put the trunks down again when they spot the price tag! Trunks can be quite expensive, no matter what the size. They're frequently used in home decor, which serves to support the outrageous cost.

This sample is a tabletop model, slim yet large enough to hold numerous items. Its rectangular shape is decorated in a sturdy, beige cloth covered in wine bottle shapes, wine-associated names, and grapes. The interior is beige in color and smooth to the touch. A lock is fastened to the front. The trunk's corners are protected with metal bumpers secured with studs, but don't let that fool you into thinking it can't be dented. I've traveled with this trunk to conduct gift basket seminars and packed it in bubble wrap in my luggage. It now has a permanent airline souvenir—a small impression within the gold plating.

You can choose to cut floral foam to fit the trunk's bottom or add two sheets of packing paper to fill the interior before adding shred. Green-colored shred was chosen because it highlights the green colors within the trunk's design. Many products fit into this container. Included are corn snacks, seasoned nuts, rum cake,

With their spacious interiors, trunks can hold a great many gifts.

chicken noodle soup, Thanks a Million cake, chocolate pasta, and raspberry dessert topping. One pick was added in the opening between the cake and dessert sauce.

The cake's theme, Thanks a Million, dictates the reason for this gift. It's a special design that's used to impress the receiver. I created several trunk designs for an executive vice president of a pharmaceutical firm. He asked that each gift be hand-delivered to the homes and temporary apartments of job candidates who were recommended by high-level contacts. An accountant also asked for such a gift to be delivered to her best client.

You may not work with high-powered clients, but you will find reasons to create trunk gift designs. For example, I have a friend who loves scuba diving, and I could

think of no better container for her birthday than a trunk. I chose one in a square shape and a design similar to the one shown on the previous page. Then I transformed the empty vessel into a sunken treasure masterpiece. She screamed with delight as she opened the lid to see two handfuls of coins and other gold-wrapped chocolates, several white chocolate starfish, a pair of goggles, a spyglass, a fantasy pirate's map, an eye patch, Mardi Gras–type necklaces, and miniature sunken ships (the type used in fish tanks). Can you think of a similar design that someone will love receiving?

Decorative trunks are found in a variety of colors and styles. Many times you'll find them at yard sales and other low-cost events where someone else's trash becomes your newfound treasure.

This swirl-pattern box makes a lovely container—but you can also flip it upside down and use it as a base for a tower creation.

GOURMET TOWER

Up to now you've seen each container filled from the inside. The vessel is packed with floral form or paper, and products are mounted in place surrounded by coordinating embellishments. But not every container has to be filled on the inside. Why not flip a container, using the outside bottom as a base to build a gift upward in pyramid style? That's what's done with this beautiful laminated box with cutout handles on each side.

The gold-swirled design on an off-white background reflects a celebration or cheerful scene. It's a great container for a basic design, but when you flip it over, the pattern becomes a focal point and gets the attention it deserves. This technique is part of the "thinking out of the box" routine that designers are faced with every day when asked to create something different. Items that would normally be added on the inside are stacked atop each other, and the gift is enclosed in cellophane and topped with a dazzling bow. What person wouldn't love to receive a tower of treats?

A rum cake is the first and widest item, sitting directly on the box. Its goldenrod packaging makes a beautiful contrast to the box. Next is a can of spicy snack mix. The can's sky-blue label works for this towering gift because there's a hint of blue on

To create a tower, look for gifts in graduating sizes: large, small, smaller.   *Stack the products skyscraper-style.*

Add two or more glue dots between the products.   *The completed Gourmet Tower.*

the rum cake package. Last is a can of lemon cookies. Its label is also lemon, which matches the border around the rum cake's box. Each product's package is smaller than the one just below. That's a necessity to create this gift. Color matching, though mentioned here, isn't as important.

Boxes, bags, and tins can be of differing shapes, so long as each sits evenly atop the rest. The taller the gift, the more valuable it's perceived as being. Don't, however, stack a design to rival the Empire State Building! Three or four items are best. If you create anything taller, the gift might become unmanageable as you attempt to close it within cellophane or shrink wrap. Unfortunately, no basket bag is tall enough to enclose this design.

Place at least two glue dots between the top and bottom of each product. This includes the container and the rum cake just above it. The area around the bottom of each product doesn't have to stay bare. Some designers twist garland around each product's base, and some leave it clean. Before wrapping the design, you may consider adding shred on the container, directly around the first product.

Have your bow ready before closing the design. A true designer won't measure, cut, and apply cellophane only to release a perfect wrap to make a bow. Cut the cellophane so that a 3- to 5-inch width remains on each side. That will ensure that there's enough room for proper closure. Seal the cellophane with tape on either side, and close on top with a bow. Extra curling ribbon looks great, or you can add long tails to the bow to drape into place on each side of the tower. Glue dots help to position the wavy ribbon.

The same design can be created using a thin flat base such as an inverted silver tray (any size, with or without handles), a tray table or serving tray, or a cutting board. Another option is to anchor your tower of gifts with a gift or food product, leaving a tray or box completely out of the design. If that were the case here, the rum cake would serve as the base.

My Get-Well gifts feature a square, 500-piece puzzle box as the base, with other busy-hands items decreasing in size stacked atop. The last item is usually a cup and saucer with a small package of cookies and the recipient's favorite beverage in the cup. Stacking is an easy process. The main drawback is finding items that both stack together and match the receiver's preferences. Still, given all the products available to you, it shouldn't be difficult to strike a balance between the two.

Practice making your first tower gift with a maximum of three items, including the container if you choose to add one. You may love the design so much that you'll decide to keep it instead of giving it away.

The Latte Tower design.

A rear view of the Latte Tower's top, with a favorite beverage tucked in back.

Mardi Gras beads make a colorful addition, if you like, for a female recipient.

LATTE TOWER

Small cups and saucers aren't the only containers that work well inside baskets or as stand-alone gifts. Many designers incorporate oversized cup sets within tower gifts or as a single gift option for a person who requires extra pizzazz as part of the presentation. Latte is associated with larger cups. Originating in France, it's a drink made with espresso and steamed milk and served in an oversized cup.

The sample gift depicted here is another tower option. It combines a latte cup and saucer, a tin container of dipping pretzels and mustard, key lime straw snacks, cappuccino, and two flavored spoons. You can turn the saucer upside down to create a base, as done here, or leave the saucer so that the edges are pointing upward. Either method works, because the saucer is solid green on both sides. The black-and-white-checked tin sits atop the saucer and is easy to position.

A regular-sized cup would work above the tin, but this oversized cup adds balance to the entire design. The box of key lime straws is inserted first into the cup. White and gold-colored shred is tucked in the spaces between the cup and box. Flavored spoons are inserted on the left, followed by a package of cappuccino at the back and small pick on the right. Mardi Gras–type beads add interest around the cup but aren't needed if you can't find a source for them. In addition, you might want to skip them if a man is to receive this gift.

As with the tall tower design, glue dots are secured between the cup, saucer, and tin. The key lime straw box is tall, eliminating the need for packing paper or floral foam within the cup. Close this design in cellophane or shrink wrap. Your bow choice will depend on the person to receive this design. A green or black-and-white bow fits for a man or woman. In addition, a combination yellow-and-green bow works for a woman.

This is a typical all-occasion gift that's simple to make. The tin adds height, but don't overlook other items. For instance, a boxed cake, a container of cookies, or a tin of chocolates each makes wonderful substitutes. Latte cups are available in many colors. They are found in supermarkets and specialty stores and sometimes at discounters. I've seen these cup combinations for a low as $3.00—a terrific price that rivals what some wholesalers charge their retail customers.

Keep this gift in mind whenever you want to make a presentation that towers above all others.

The Cup-and-Saucer design.

These chocolate lover's gifts are supported in the cup with skewers. Any number of treats can be substituted.

CUP AND SAUCER

A card store owner asked me to come to her store to develop ideas to sell her cups and saucers. She had recently moved twenty-five sets to the clearance area, and they still weren't selling. It was late April, a great time to think about Mother's Day gifts. So I turned these beautifully designed sets decorated with pink and yellow rosebuds into gifts for moms.

Hard candies available in the store were gathered in handfuls and wrapped in cellophane closed with one string of curling ribbon. The candies were inserted into the cups. All twenty-five cups and saucers were wrapped in cellophane and topped with a small bow. The store owner positioned the newly packaged gifts around the checkout counter. Within three days everything was sold, and the store owner was surprised at how simple packaging turned tea cups and saucers into an instant, full-priced success.

We often pass cup and saucer sets in clearance areas and at flea markets, never seeing the potential to make a thoughtful gift for an aunt, grandmother, or longtime friend. These sets are extremely easy to turn into gift items. You can use snacks, candies, small gifts, and beverages to create a beautiful product in a matter of minutes.

In the design shown on the facing page, glue dots are used to anchor the cup and saucer together. Tissue paper lines the back of the cup. A small piece of floral foam is covered with tissue paper and inserted into the cup. Orange-colored shred is tucked into the cup and around the foam. Skewers are added to the back of the chocoholic's cake, cocoa mix, and chocolate-turtle-flavored coffee. This anchoring method is discussed in chapter 4 (see page 34). Each product is added to the cup, starting from the back. When the items are stabilized, place star spray at the back. A flavored spoon fills a slightly open space on the right. Small basket bags will create a snug fit for this set, or you can choose cellophane.

Cups and saucers create a favorite basketless design that takes about five minutes to complete from start to finish. The set's pattern reflects the recipient's tastes, and so do the contents. Cookies, biscotti, chocolates, jelly beans, tea, crackers, nuts, and candies are some of the options that fit into this petite pair. Individually wrapped hard candies can be placed on the saucer around the cup's bottom. These candies don't need anchoring. Each can move freely in the small space between the cup and cellophane.

Floral foam and skewers aren't requirements when working with a cup and saucer. Shred can be tucked between tall, slim items that extend above the rim such as shown in the mug design (see page 140). At this point it will be difficult to resist picking up every cup-and-saucer set sold at yard sales. But try not to buy them all unless you're selling them to a retailer who's looking for outside creativity.

Mug I. A personalized mug creates a thoughtful custom gift. Here it sits atop a clam dip kit.

Some products here are nestled inside the mug, while others rest horizontally atop its rim.

Picks and ting-ting at the back complete the design.

MUGS

Who among us doesn't have assorted mugs in our home waiting to be filled with coffee, tea, flavored spoons, cookies, and other small goodies? Mugs are incredibly easy to design. This no-fuss container makes a perfect thank-you, welcome, or appreciation gift. The main consideration is finding items tall enough to fit both inside and above the rim, or adding attractive items that fit horizontally across the rim. Two mugs are shown here to depict both design types.

The white mug is personalized with the name GENESIS. Such mugs are available in variety stores and are the basis for creating a customized gift specifically for birthdays and thank-yous. Red-colored shred fills the mug and stabilizes two extra items. Flavored sugar, the front product, is placed in the mug. A Post-it notepad and small tin of chocolates sit horizontally across the mug. Glue dots are used between each product as support. A package of cappuccino, which is tall enough to extend into the mug, is added behind the chocolates. An iced-tea spoon peeks above the cappuccino. Two picks and two pieces of ting-ting are added to the back, and the design is complete.

Mugs are often the gift of choice for

Mug II. The special frosted mug used here keeps beverages cold for hours.

A small assortment of treats is tucked inside this mug.

You can add embellishments after the gift is wrapped. Here, a bow and flower add cheer.

supervisors who buy Administrative Professionals Day gifts for the office support staff team. Cookies, coffee, and flowers are bundled together. A small pick stating HAPPY ADMINISTRATIVE PROFESSIONALS DAY, which looks similar to the HAPPY NEW YEAR'S pick in chapter 9 (see page 88), is placed in front before wrapping.

Not all products will sit as steadily as the chocolates and notepad. Each is wide enough to fit across the mug's rim, and the extra support provided by the cappuccino, flavored coffee, and glue dots ensures that these products won't move before closing the gift in a basket bag or cellophane.

Consider placing an item directly below the mug. The square clam dip kit package shown under the white mug is slightly larger and fits perfectly. Designers often add something special in this manner when a client requests a unique product that is too large to fit within the mug. Glue dots secure the two products together.

This mug is personalized, but your selection may not be. A cup, as used in the previous Cup-and-Saucer design, or the snowman mug in chapter 9 (see page 102), makes a terrific gift, as does any of the assortment of unused mugs in your kitchen cabinets, basement, or attic.

Mugs are available in all shapes and sizes, including the frosty mug shown in the second design. Distilled water is trapped within this mug's circular wall. It's placed in the freezer so that the water freezes and keeps a beverage cold for hours. All the products in this design are contained within the mug. Green shred can be seen through the mug's transparent design. The shortest item, microwave popcorn, is in front. A beef stick is in the middle, and two chocolate-covered pretzel rods are in back.

Two embellishments are added. You don't, however, need a variety of picks for each mug. Some designs look stunning without extra flowers and curls. Look at your finished mug before adding to the cost with embellishments.

The frosty mug is wrapped with cellophane. Its sides are closed in the triangular format. A bow made from metallic chenille ribbon and enhanced with a flower pick brightens the look. The metallic chenille is wired, which makes curling and shaping the bow's loops and ends a snap.

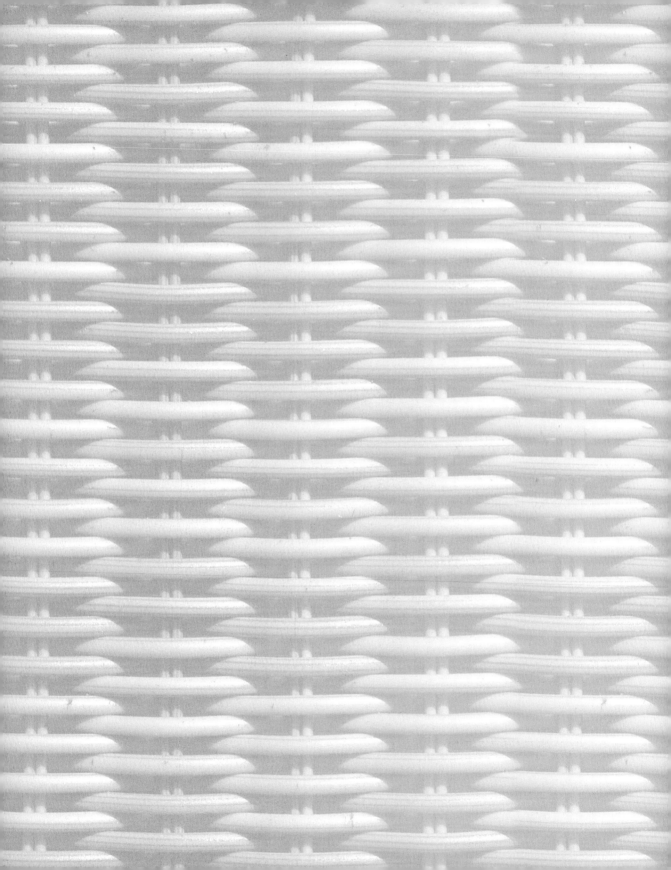

PART THREE
Beyond the Basics

A portable supply kit will allow you to perform all sorts of gift basket first aid.

Chapter 12

QUICK FIXES
Don't Get Mad, Get Creative!

Gift baskets and nonbasket designs provide a wide variety of options for all-occasion gift giving. You've learned new ways to create baskets, satisfied your curiosity about how designs are prepared, and seen many options to build gifts when baskets aren't available or needed.

When you visit a store and see beautiful gift baskets on shelves and pedestals, you're looking at the finished product. There's no indication of the problems that may have occurred during construction. All types of design problems arise for beginners and experts. Most situations have easy solutions, and others are so severe that you must start again.

In chapter 3 you learned about cutting floral foam and the consequences of cutting the foam too short. However, adding U-shaped pins between two bricks adds to the length, thereby solving the short-brick problem. Chapter 6 explained how to use a pick to mask a hole caused by excess heat on shrink wrap. What happens if you

cut your cellophane so short that the height above the design looks stubby? Can it be fixed, or should you discard the cello? This chapter provides solutions for this and other everyday problems.

SUPPLY KIT

Gift baskets may be a hobby or may be a profession for you, but in either case it's a skill you take very seriously. You might lead a PTA fund-raiser that calls for a hundred baskets and mugs to be auctioned during a black-tie charity event. As an office manager, perhaps you'll assist in creating fifty gift baskets for distribution to the most productive employees. Or you may be part of an awards committee and be called upon to make twenty-five gift baskets filled with donated items.

Whatever the case, the baskets must be transported from one location to another. Anything can and will happen between points A and B. Cellophane tears, balloons break, and ribbons tangle. You won't be ready for everything, but you can arm yourself against small problems.

How? Professional gift basket designers create what they call a *supply kit* that stays by their side in the workspace and travels with them by car to client destinations. This kit is a personal version of a doctor's bag and is as necessary to today's designers as eating and sleeping. It contains the basic supplies that turn a near disaster into success. A wire caddy coated in heavy white plastic is shown as an example. It includes:

- Scissors
- Wire cutters
- Glue dots
- Transparent tape
- One sheet of tissue paper
- One basket bag or 3 feet of cellophane
- Two handfuls of shred
- One spool of curling ribbon
- One star spray
- One additional enhancement

Designers also add foam, skewers, balloons, and accompanying supplies (cups and sticks) and extra bows. The exact contents of your kit will depend on what's important for your designs. Careful monitoring of the kit is also important. If the transparent tape expires and you forget to replenish it, the kit will be useless. The same is true for other supplies that you'll use up over time.

Each kit's contents will change periodically. A designer who's delivering a baby basket with yellow shred will replace the kit's green shred with yellow or may travel with several shred colors and check the kit before leaving. This kit is helpful on the road and also comes in handy if you design in one room but need a few supplies in another. Why pack yards of supplies when a few inches will do?

There's no need to buy a specific container to create a supply kit. A basket that's too old or unattractive is a good candidate. The same can be said for an old toolbox or another handled caddy. Shoe boxes and other cardboard containers don't work as well because they neither contain a handle nor recover from bad weather.

CELLOPHANE

Now that you've learned how to arm yourself for unexpected rips and tears, let's see how to put these tools to use. We'll start with cellophane problems.

Adding More on Top

Here are the supplies you'll need:

- Cellophane
- Curling ribbon
- Scissors

A tall fan of cellophane above the closing bow always raises the basket's perceived value. Cutting the wrong length or a sudden tear in the cello creates a stubby

1. *Problem: Baskets need a tall fan of cellophane above the closing bow. This stubby top looks out of balance.*

2. *Solution: Cut an extra piece of cellophane and gather it in your hand.*

3. *Place the extra cellophane around the basket's short top.*

4. *Tie ribbon around the basket's neck where the old and new cello meet.*

5. *The ribbon effectively joins the two pieces of cello.*

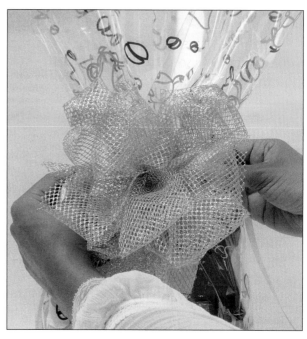

6. *Add a bow to hide any extra cello.*

7. *Trim the cellophane evenly at the top.*

8. *Your fix is complete.*

top that appears in disproportion to the design. The solution isn't difficult to master, but you must exercise patience to fix this pesky problem.

Keep the short cello above the design together with curling ribbon, but remove the bow if tied in place. Cut a piece of curling ribbon approximately 2 feet long. Put it on the table, but keep it close to add around the design's neck. Cut a piece of cellophane across the roll and about 4 inches wide. Put the roll aside.

Using one hand, gather the entire cellophane together at the bottom of one end, leaving approximately ½ inch below your hand. The cellophane above your hand resembles a fan topping.

Using both hands, place the gathered cellophane evenly around the short cello on the design.The new cellophane will encircle the short piece. Hold it in place, and tie the curling ribbon around the neck where the old and new cello meet. The curling ribbon should be placed below the ribbon, enclosing the old cello. This provides the new cello with extra support. Tie the bow around the new cellophane. The bow should cover the additional cello that hangs below the curling ribbon. If not, carefully snip the visible cellophane to shorten as needed.

If the new cello is uneven at the top, bring it together and cut it in a semicircle. Expand the cellophane on each side. The problem is solved.

Tip: Some designers add an extra fan topper onto their basket. This is done in the same way as described above. Instead of one cello color, two separate but coordinated toppers appear above the basket's neck. For example, if a basket is covered with plain cellophane, you can add printed cello around the plain wrap for a decorative topper.

1. Problem: Cellophane tears easily, especially when you insert embellishments from outside.

Patching Tears

You'll need these supplies:

- Cellophane
- Transparent tape
- Scissors

There are cellophane tears that can be patched and others that require the cello to be replaced. You will know which can be saved and which must be discarded according to the patch results.

Cellophane has a mind of its own. It usually doesn't tear, unless pulled, pricked

or provoked—any or all of which are inevitable when you wrap a package. Problems can occur when inserting enhancements from the outside. For example, you add a pick or star spray by first deciding where the enhancement will rest, then placing a small piece of transparent tape where the enhancement will pierce the cello. Cut the cellophane with scissors by pinching the tape on the cellophane and making a small cut, then insert the enhancement through the cello and into the basket.

Transparent tape prevents the cello-

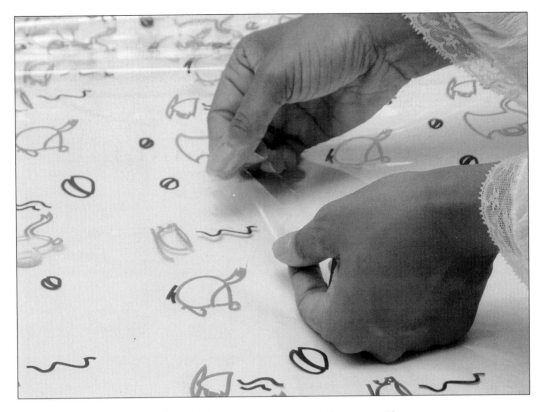

2. Solution: Repair the cello by applying transparent tape to the reverse side.

phane's tear from migrating. New designers, however, often forget to add tape or snip beyond the tape and onto the cello, which causes irreparable damage if not caught quickly.

The best way to repair a cellophane tear is by applying transparent tape, preferably on the cello's opposite side. This may require you to remove the bow, smooth the cellophane onto a flat surface, and tape as needed. Turn the taped cello toward the back of the design before reapplying it around the basket.

If the rip is in front and repairable, some designers add glue dots on top of the tape and press flower petals or greenery on the dots. This solution isn't always workable, though; it depends on the location of the tear and its length. Still, try it before starting over.

Tip: If you replace the cellophane, store the old piece for use as a fan topper or as filler material within another basket or container.

1. Problem: Star spray can prove difficult. Pulling on the stars, for instance, may dislodge a piece.

ENHANCEMENTS

When working with enhancements, you're likely to face two problems again and again: broken star spray and torn ribbons. Here are two solutions that might prove helpful.

Reviving Star Spray

You'll need:

- Basket or container design
- Star spray parts
- Scissors or skewer (optional)

You learned how to add star spray to a basket in chapter 5 (see page 38). Star spray consists of four parts:

- Multiple blades of onion grass
- Three wires decorated with stars
- One stem
- A center casing that holds it all together

This enhancement is purchased tall and straight, but the grass and wired stars are curled with scissors before basket insertion.

Pulling a blade of onion grass might cause it to break, but that's not a

2. Solution: If this happens, use spare pieces as embellishments in their own right.

problem. There's always a piece of torn grass still wrapped in the casing. The end is curled, along with the remaining onion grass, and it's ready for placement. The three pieces of wired stars are curled around a pencil (for a thin curl), Magic Marker (for a thick curl), or your finger. The wound curl is pulled upward to extend its height.

Pulling the wired stars may cause the piece to become dislodged. That's when your ingenuity tells you it's better to use the piece than throw it away. Remnants are easily added within baskets. Designers place these renegade parts between products or wind them around handles. The stars and wire are brightly colored, creating a decorative appearance wherever they're added.

Tip: Wired stars are an attractive addition around the neck of a bottle or mug handle.

Lengthening a Bow's Ribbon

Here's what you'll need:

- Bow
- Curling ribbon
- Scissors

The expression *Haste makes waste* must have been coined by a person securing a bow on a basket. Rushing to finish a design usually results in a mini disaster. Half the time it's stabilizing a product, and the other half it's a piece of curling ribbon breaking from a bow. This is not to say that ribbons break often, but when it happens, the situation is frustrating. One bright spot is that when the curling ribbon breaks, the bow is usually left undamaged and won't unravel to cause new problems.

Your solution is simple. Tying a piece of curling ribbon to the broken end is one option. However, the broken piece might be so short that it's impossible to do so. The better option is to thread a new strand of curling ribbon in the bow's midsection.

Use your scissors to cut the remaining strand of ribbon. Next, look at the bow to determine the best place to add the curling ribbon. It will be inserted between the loops. Thread the ribbon into place, bringing the ends toward the back. If done correctly, the insertion point of the ribbon will be masked by the bow's loops. If not, look for a new insertion point and reinsert the ribbon.

Center the bow onto the basket, and tie the new curling ribbon strands around the neck. Curl the ends with scissors.

You'll encounter other snags while designing gift baskets. Most problems won't extend beyond the situations shown here, but by the time more advanced problems occur, you'll know how to turn a crisis into victory.

1. *Problem: Many designers have known the frustration of seeing a ribbon break from a bow, leaving only one strand to attach the bow to the gift basket.*

2. Solution: Cut the remaining ribbon with scissors.

3. Start over again by finding the bow's midsection.

4. Thread a new ribbon through the middle and bring both ends to the back.

5. The ribbon's insertion point should be masked by the bow's loops.

Flora Brown's Garden Helper basket.

Chapter 13

DESIGNERS AND THEIR GIFT BASKETS

Regional Pros Share Their Inspiration

I travel from east to west to conduct seminars at industry shows and public events and meet no fewer than 1,000 gift basket designers each year. Some seminar attendees are just considering making gift baskets. Others have already started designing. Then there are the seasoned professionals who greet me as though I'm an old friend, whether or not we've met in the past.

Designers at every stage of the craft constantly teach me something new. Their spirit and enthusiasm tell me that gift baskets aren't just a product; they are a way of life that individuals proudly embrace as their everyday work. It's the love of the craft that keeps us all designing.

The four designers you're about to meet embody the creative spirit that gift basket makers share around the world. Let me introduce you to these regional pros and let's take a close look at some of their most successful basket designs to date.

FLORA BROWN:
Gift Baskets by Flora, Anaheim, California

On a typical trip to Southern California, I expect three things: (1) the sun, (2) traffic congestion, and (3) two incredibly styled gift baskets waiting for my arrival. Flora is the designing diva that I aspire to become. I pause to admire her work; then she introduces me to the Garden Helper and the California Garden.

Flora names her baskets because it gives each a personality, and that's what her clients love. Realtors are especially fond of these designs, which they buy in bulk for their homeowners and sellers to thank them for their business. After ten years of designing, Flora has tapped into Realtors' referral markets, and that means lots of repeat customers. It's one reason why this award-winning designer's business continues to thrive. Flora is gifted with a visual imagination, which allows her to create a

A ribbon secures the garden gloves to the watering can.

Flora Brown has mastered the art of securing products without glue dots and tape.

Flora's California Garden basket combines useful garden products—including spades and a bird house—in a surprising base.

This design comes alive with the addition of moss, pine, and floral embellishments.

gift basket in her mind before she starts working with her hands. She made the Garden Helper for Realtors who prefer out-of-the-ordinary baskets. It includes a watering can; kneeling pad; garden tools; cocoa briquette; garden plaque; and Bath Buddies, a bar of glycerin soap with an embedded animal shape. There's also a birdhouse pick and birdhouse wind chime for hanging in the garden. The wind chime is weighty, a prerequisite for most items to pass inspection for this design.

A waterless hand cleaner lets homeowners refresh without water as they take pause after gardening. A bow secures the garden gloves onto the can. Plaid and white ribbons inscribed with WELCOME add warmth.

Under this bundle of beauty are layers of newsprint and shred, but there's less support on top. Flora has mastered a design style that eliminates the need for glue dots and tape. That keeps her design time to a minimum and lets the receiver take the gift apart faster. She does, however, encourage beginners to "take advantage of glue dots and tape if needed." The finished product is shrink-wrapped quickly so that the products stay in place.

Flora loves to use enhancements. She says it's the "key to bringing the basket alive. Adding enhancements and a bow will separate you from an amateur." She suggests buying quality products that look real and using these items sparingly. Most of her enhancements are bought after the holidays when deep discounts prevail.

Another of Flora's top sellers is the California Garden basket. It's one of her "wild baskets" because "it's so creative and wows people." A water hose acts as the foundation. It's exactly as it was when initially purchased, wound together and secured with plastic ties.

The inner cavity is filled with newsprint and shred. A birdhouse is positioned on top and gently pushed downward so it doesn't wobble. Recipients are elated with the shovels added on either side, sunblock, garden book, Bath Buddies soap with butterfly, hummingbird nectar (bird food), plant seeds, and hand sanitizer. This design is wrapped twice before delivery, with shrink wrap on the inside and cellophane on top. The double coating stabilizes the package and provides a soft outer covering.

Flora suggests that you "bring your designs alive with something living." As an example, she glued a faux bird to the top of the house and added moss and pine embellishments that don't resemble Christmas decorations.

Flora's support team includes part-time staffers and family members. They take turns in the private studio, designing and delivering or snipping ribbon and clipping parts. This handy work keeps downtime to a minimum and the studio buzzing with activity. Her newest venture, www.Gift BasketBusinessWorld.com, provides new and veteran designers with tips and resource materials to create beautifully styled gift baskets of their own.

Elaine Essary's gift basket contains enough treats to feed a group. The basket is topped with a large cellophane fan and a paper bow.

This basket includes premium snacks, such as white chocolate popcorn and chocolate-covered grahams.

ELAINE ESSARY:
The Basket Bar, Calumet City, Illinois

One look at Elaine, and I could see a dynamo in the making. With just a few years of business under her belt, the fire in her eyes still flickers with determination to make her mark. Elaine started her business in December 2001. She worked as a recruitment manager/corporate trainer but was laid off due to downsizing after the 9/11 tragedy. Elaine began making gift baskets for family and friends. "People loved them," she says, and that gave her the inspiration to consider a new career.

Elaine was determined to start with as much knowledge as possible, so she invested three months into research, reading books on what it's like to become a designer. She also purchased general business books. "I put lots of dollars into it." Elaine visited gift basket message boards on the Internet for ideas and insight. She soon registered her business name and began attending trade shows to

Elaine anchors the tallest products with skewers and glue dots.

buy products at wholesale cost. The purchases are stored in her garage, and the car no longer has a home. But the trade-off has been a business that offers impressive rewards.

The featured basket contains enough goods for an entire group to enjoy. Packing paper cushions the bottom before a layer of beige, green, and burgundy shred is added. When choosing products, Elaine buys a variety of items with varying heights to create a well-rounded basket. This design includes truffles, shortbread cookies, caramels, peanuts, hard candy, a snack mix, cookies, popcorn, coffee, and iced tea. She uses skewers and glue dots to anchor her products. You may be tempted to make a meal of these goodies, but when you're in business, that's not a good idea. "It's money," says Elaine, "so I don't even think about eating it."

The cost of picks and flowers adds up, and Elaine prefers to spend money on foods and snacks. Two basket products requested most often are white chocolate popcorn and chocolate-covered graham crackers. Items made in Illinois top Elaine's must-have list, because she has easy access to manufacturers when she needs to fill an order quickly. But quickness is balanced with a double check of expiration dates. Elaine monitors all products for freshness to ensure that nothing stale is mistakenly added.

The cellophane fan in the center is made with a Bowdabra machine and then tied to a tall, plastic stick. Elaine ties it on with curling ribbon along with a paper bow for added enhancement. She chooses cellophane to cover her designs rather than shrink wrap.

Eighty-five percent of her sales are to corporate customers, some of which are mortgage companies that Elaine finds through her local newspaper. Other sales are Internet orders placed by customers who visit her Web site. Elaine's bank is also a client. She combined the bank's imprinted mug with coffee and biscotti and also imprinted its name on ribbon using a machine. She walked in and presented the bank's president with the mug. The two began talking, and Elaine learned that the president planned to send gifts and baskets to customers. This interaction netted the account for Elaine.

Not being content to rest on her laurels, Elaine joined several organizations, including Business Networking International (BNI) and a home builders association. Elaine doesn't fear talking about her business to new people. Her motto is, *The worst they can say is no.*

Savvy designers know how to recruit free help. Elaine found her marketing intern at a local college. He helps her develop marketing plans, which earns him college credits. It's a great arrangement for both parties.

Elaine's husband recently retired from the police force, and they will soon move to another Chicago suburb that's home to the type of individuals she currently serves. That will decrease her time on the road delivering gift baskets. She hopes to also increase her client list.

Elaine urges anyone who wants to make gift baskets to "do your homework." It will help limit mistakes and keep the fire in your eyes burning for years.

Lise Schleicher transformed a slow-moving millennium container into her popular Puttin' on the Ritz basket. The platinum-colored fabric and bow create a clean, sophisticated look.

LISE SCHLEICHER:
BasketWorks,
Northbrook, Illinois

There are two choices after six years in business: You sink or you swim. Where does Lise Schleicher stand? Let's just say she's a mermaid with a buoyant personality to match.

Lise opened her gift basket business in 1997 after searching for a career that matched her skills. She worked in retail for two years and a floral shop for four years. That's where she learned to make bows and much more. Color matching was another requirement. Today all this knowledge helps

her make smart inventory choices. For example, she prefers natural-colored baskets, which she sprays white for baby baskets and gold or silver for holiday gifts. Prepainted baskets offer Lise less versatility. "You can do many things and create unique themes using the color white as the backdrop," she explains.

It's no wonder that her featured basket is white and black. Packing peanuts are added inside this tuxedo container. The peanuts are placed into tissue paper and rolled for stabilization. Smoked salmon pâté, chocolate-covered pretzels, cookies, and other confections are paired. Lise uses few embellishments in her baskets. The platinum-colored bow and matching fabric are all that's needed to create an elegant image.

This design recently won an award at a gift basket convention, but it wasn't always a winner. Lise purchased these containers for the millennium, but they didn't sell. She would have been stuck with unmovable inventory had she not considered an alternative use. Lise searched for ribbon and fabric that would transform the container and called the design Puttin' on the Ritz. The new image created hefty sales. It sells not only for everyday occasions but also for weddings, anniversaries, thank-you gifts, and to corporations that love it because they like the design's "clean look."

Lise's biggest customers are home builders, a machinery firm, a home painter, Chicago's United Center, and the Schubert Theater, a client she recently acquired. The latter orders gift baskets for VIPs, headliners, and supporters. Lise enjoys serving clients in different industries, terming it as "being all over the map." The variety keeps her designs fresh and innovative.

Some clients request ad specialty items, such as mugs, in their baskets. That's the reason Lise maintains a broad inventory, which includes many containers. Client favorites include thank-you and get well baskets. Snelling Personnel is one client that requires her to incorporate its colors into each basket sent to clients. A ribbon imprinter is invaluable in providing custom ribbon in a flash.

Containers are important, but Lise estimates that 75 percent of her sales are baskets, especially for new babies. Approximately 50 percent of sales are food baskets that incorporate themed cookies, chocolate chip cookies, snack mixes, kosher items, tortilla chips, dipping pretzels and mustards, tea, mulling cider, dips, and crackers. Small gift books, coffee, jelly beans, and white chocolate bark are some of the more popular inventory.

Lise creates twelve new designs a year, and everything is a custom creation. One item will strike her, and that's when the idea for a whole package begins. Last year copper ribbon was high on Lise's list. This year silk flowers are the target. "I find something—coffee, flowers—and it sets me off."

Lise has a bachelor's degree in business management and a master's in labor relations. Her sister, Caren, is the marketing guru who helps Lise develop products and services that spread the word about her business. This includes making calls to potential customers and assisting Lise at expos and open house events. Lise and Caren also mail specially printed postcards to prospects and customers.

Because of her business background, Lise knew that she had to start networking to sell her designs, so she joined a networking group three months after opening for business. She's now a member of three groups and a board of directors group.

Lise sums up why swimming to success is her only option: "I'm a business-person first, creative person second, and it all balances out."

A signature gift basket by Marie Pessolano and Marian Donnelly.

MARIE PESSOLANO AND MARIAN DONNELLY:
The Giving Basket, Randolph, New Jersey

It was 9:00 A.M. on Tuesday when Marie Pessolano, co-owner of The Giving Basket, greeted me at the door. Then the phone rang, and it rang many times during my stay. And the fax started buzzing. Orders were everywhere. Marie and co-owner Marian Donnelly are very busy, and it's only mid-August. Most designers should be so lucky, but this is no overnight success story. It's taken them long hours of work and dedication to grow from being competitors to becoming a dynamic duo.

Marie and Marian own The Giving Basket in Randolph, New Jersey, which opened its doors in 1989 with Marian at the helm before her partnership with Marie in 1992. You walk into a showroom upon entering, then walk past several offices and a sizable workroom large enough for numerous employees creating custom gifts in assembly style. The back opens into a cavernous space to house inventory. Baskets, containers, shred, foods, and gifts line shelves awaiting their turn for inclusion. Stairs are tucked in a corner leading to an upstairs loft with a large design space, photo studio, and more products arranged on shelves.

The duo created every basket in the early years, convincing anyone within earshot to help, especially during the holidays. But a turning point was near. Christmas sales were terrific, but both agree that the workload was "out of hand." Orders were massive, and they worked most nights until 4:00 A.M. Marie and Marian believed that if they survived Christmas, they could do anything.

The Giving Basket now employs eight to twenty workers, depending on the season. A permanent staff takes care of the daily designs and backroom operations (checking merchandise, record keeping, and the like). High school students are recruited for holiday support. They come with mature minds and recognize the meaning of working together to get the job done. If the students are also athletes, all the better. These superjocks turn the work into a contest, and the orders are prepared faster than a 50-yard dash.

Individuals frequently buy their designs, but to Fortune 500 companies, the baskets are an investment. Marian and Marie's most profitable work is created by setting up corporate programs. Their clients' headquarters and branch offices are on schedules to receive baskets for clients, employees, and referrals. Productivity, baby, sympathy, and other baskets are selected by these giants to keep their businesses healthy. Marie networks and makes the presentations, while Marian keeps the office running like a well-oiled machine. Partners often work this way, though

Cookies, jams, crackers, cheese, and popcorn add up to a delightful basket of treats.

Marie says that Marian is "much better at selling than she thinks."

It didn't take much selling to convince this pair to join forces. In 1987 Marie began making gift baskets at home, and Marian opened a gift basket shop in 1989 while working part time as a nurse. Marian soon found the shop to be overwhelming and decided to sell her inventory. One look through the yellow pages led her to Marie. While talking shop, they found similarities in their work styles. A partnership was formed. One year after teaming up in Marian's space, they moved into their current location and haven't looked back.

Marie spends time on the road meeting with prospects, who often become new clients. Awards also come in the form of accolades from peers and organizations. They graced the cover of *Gift Basket Review* in 1994 and were crowned the 1996 Small Business of the

Year by the Morris County Chamber of Commerce.

Marion and Marie see a bright future and call their business "a work in progress." Their ongoing plans include updating the Web site and streamlining most of the business. A handbook was created to guide employees on performing daily and critical tasks. It's consulted if Marion and Marie aren't available, but that doesn't mean they've grown tired of the business. "Every morning, we're still happy to be here," both say joyfully.

APPENDIX: RESOURCE LIST

Allsorts Premium Packaging

2495 Main Street, #548
Buffalo, NY 14214
(888) 565–9727
www.allsortswrap.com

An industry leader in the design and selection of soft basket wraps and bags, cutters, and related supplies. High-quality film made specifically for gift baskets.

Bay Beyond, Inc.

T/A Blue Cray Bay Co.
29368 Atlantic Drive
Melfa, VA 23410
(757) 787–3602
www.baybeyond.net

Award-winning gourmet specialty foods, indicative of the tastes and traditions of the Chesapeake Bay region. Seasoned, nuts, dip kits, marinades, and more.

Blackberry Patch & Crickle Company

P.O. Box 1639
Thomasville, GA 31799
(229) 558–9996
www.blackberrypatch.com

All-natural fruit syrups, jams, and jellies. Incredible brittle (Crickle), nuts, confectionery candy, pancake mixes, and syrups.

Chocoholics Divine Desserts

18819 East Highway 88
Clements, CA 95227-0730
(209) 931–5188
www.gourmetchocolate.com

Premium gourmet chocolate novelties and sauces. Gift packs, boxed chocolates, teaspoons, and more for gift baskets. Upscale packaging, quality products.

Creative Stuff

P.O. Box 824
Elmwood Park, NJ 07407-0824
www.bygollybygeorge.com

Whimsical gifts for baskets, including pig wands, root-head warriors, trinket boxes, aging dolls, inspirational gift tags, and an assortment of gods and goddesses.

Delicae Gourmet

1111 East Lake Drive
Tarpon Springs, FL 34689
(800) 942–2502
www.delicaegourmet.com

Award-winning coffee and tea jellies, jams, mustards, dips, rubs, vinegars, and many more condiments.

East Shore Specialty Foods

643 Cardinal Lane
P.O. Box 379
Hartland, WI 53029
(800) 236–1069
www.eastshorefoods.com

East Shore specialty pretzels and gourmet mustards are the perfect addition to any gift basket. They are available in a variety of delicious combinations.

Fleur de Lis Perfumes

26920 West Garret Drive
Calabasas, CA 91301
(800) 504–9197, code 00
www.fleurdelisperfumesstore.com

Manufactures the best in all-natural bath and body care products, original perfumes, foot care items, scrubs, and more hard-to-find fragrances and specialty items.

G.E.F. Gourmet Foods, Inc.

35584 County Road 8
Mountain Lake, MN 56159
(800) 692–6762
www.gladcorn.com

Makers of Gladcorn, "the best corn snack in America." A unique, tasty, and natural corn snack that's a hit with all ages and genders.

Gift Basket Business

P.O. Box 31, River Street Station
Paterson, NJ 07544-0031
www.giftbasketbusiness.com

Books, videos, audiotapes, free newsletter, and other resources to make gift baskets for fun or profit.

Gift Basket Business World

446 South Anaheim Hills Road
Anaheim, CA 92807
www.giftbasketbusinessworld.com

Informative booklets, free newsletter, tip sheets, and other lucrative resources for gift basket businesses on the grow.

Golden Walnut Specialty Foods, Inc.

3200 16th Street
Zion, IL 60099
(800) 843–3645
www.goldenwalnut.com

A full line of gourmet cookies, toffees, and cakes in boxes, bags, cans, and tins. Many sizes and great quality.

Highland Beef Farms

P.O. Box 2414
Reston, VA 20195
(800) 869–6320

Top-quality, shelf-stable (no refrigeration needed) meat and cheese snacks. A large variety of products that address health- and ethics-conscious consumers.

The Home Owner's Journal

2232 North 7th Street, Unit 15
Grand Junction, CO 81501
(800) 444–5450
www.homeownersjournal.com

A complete spiral-bound journal for home and apartment owners to list their home contents, valuables, repairs, and other relevant information.

Morin's Landing

P.O. Box 819
Dayton, OR 97114
(800) 945–3603
www.morinslanding.com

A wide variety of award-winning gourmet jams, mustards, sauces and mixes.

Nashville Wraps

1229 Northgate Business Parkway
Madison, TN 37115
(800) 547–9727
www.nashvillewraps.com

More than 4,000 gift basket supplies, including cellophane, basket bags, complete shrink wrap systems, boxes, ribbon, tote bags, shred, tissue paper, and more.

The Pasta Shoppe

P.O. Box 159245
Nashville, TN 37215
(800) 247–0188
www.pastashoppe.com

Great themed gift basket products, including curly and fun-shaped pastas, cookies, snack mixes, biscuits, and soup mixes.

Penelope's of Evergreen, Ltd.

P.O. Box 2863
Evergreen, CO 80437-2863
(800) 748–3443
www.penelopewinejelly.com

Six flavors of fine wine jelly in two sizes, and two sizes of fine wine sauce available in four flavors. Scone mixes and lemon curd mixes.

PurpleMoose Products

P.O. Box 7018
Golden, CO 80403
(800) 277–9135
www.purplemooseproducts.com

Makers of Celebration Cakes in short, round containers with cake mix, icing, candle, and merry maker. Add water, microwave, decorate, and celebrate.

RainCountry Naturals

P.O. Box 2125
Sisters, OR 97759
(800) 543–9133
www.raincountry.com

A full line of natural bath, beauty, and home fragrance products for all ages. Soaps, creams, lotions, room fresheners, and baby items.

Rocky Mountain Popcorn Company

520 Stacy Court, Unit D
Lafayette, CO 80026
(303) 744–8850
www.rmpopcorn.com

Gourmet ready-to-eat popcorn available in caramel, peanut butter, white cheddar, butter, cinnamon, vanilla, and low-fat caramel. Pure popcorn perfection.

Salem Baking Co.

3121 Indiana Avenue
Winston–Salem, NC 27105
(800) 274–2994
www.salembaking.com

>Sells the "world's thinnest cookies," award-winning cheese straws, and shortbread straws. Great flavor and packaging.

Stephan Enterprises, Inc.

3 Pequignot
Pierceton, IN 46562
(574) 594–2131
www.stephanenterprises.com

>Heartwarming baby gifts that are uniquely designed and moderately priced. Choose from plush toys, silver-plated gift sets, photo books and frames, bath and toiletry products.

ABOUT THE AUTHOR

Shirley George Frazier is president and founder of Sweet Survival, a retail consulting firm specializing in gift basket design, marketing, and business development. Recognized internationally as an expert on gift baskets, Shirley works with home-based designers, retail shop owners, and department store managers to help them increase their profits. She is the author of *How to Start a Home-Based Gift Basket Business,* published by The Globe Pequot Press, and writes articles for and is quoted in numerous publications. She travels extensively to speak on gift and business topics and appears on television as an industry spokesperson. Shirley lives in Paterson, New Jersey, with her husband, John; daughter, Genesis; and dog, Pepper.